# Choosing True Life

# Choosing True Life

## 30 Foundational Choices for a Life Transformed

HOLLY J. COMPTON

Published by hope*books
2217 Matthews Township Pkwy
Suite D302
Matthews, NC 28105
www.hopebooks.com

hope*books is a division of hope*media

Printed in the United States of America



First edition.
Paperback ISBN: 979-8-89185-364-5
Hardcover ISBN: 979-8-89185-365-2
Ebook ISBN: 979-8-89185-366-9
Library of Congress Number: 2026933911

hb
hope*books
hopebooks.com
Because the world needs your hope-filled words now more than ever.

# Endorsements

Powerful, practical, and beautifully written—this book is life-changing. It will transform how you see yourself and the world around you.

Robert Walker
Senior Pastor, The Prayer Room Church,
Conroe, Texas

Like the wedding miracle in John 2, Holly shows us that Jesus is present, ready to take the ordinary "water" of our daily lives—our routines, our struggles, and our decisions—and transform it into the **fine wine** of a life fully lived. This transformation is not relegated to a single, dramatic event, but is found in the **daily, practical decision** to walk intimately with Christ. This book is a catalyst for **Christ-powered transformation.**

Jon Adams
Founding Pastor, The Vine Community Church,
Cumming, Georgia

*Choosing True Life* is a must-read for anyone stepping into their newfound faith and a refreshing reminder for seasoned believers. My friend Holly beautifully captures the life-giving truth of God's Word with clarity, insight, and heartfelt conviction, illuminating the vital foundations of the Christian walk. Don't miss this easy-to-read yet truly life-changing work.

Matt Brinkley<br>Founder, PACT Ministry

*Choosing True Life* is Holly's honest and engaging spiritual journal of what it looks like to find, follow, and flourish in life with Christ, in both the good and challenging times. But it's so much more than telling her story; she reveals the truths from the Scripture she learned that helped her and you, the reader, today, be transformed by the Spirit into a new person who makes a kingdom difference in their world. These truths are not quick fixes, but daily choices, centered on Christ, that give you a life map on the road to kingdom living—A life-long journey. *Choosing True Life* will encourage, inspire, and instruct you to a more meaningful life of following Christ.

Dr. Steve Norris<br>Director of Discipleship at<br>Grace School of Theology, Adjunct Professor<br>Retired Pastor of Discipleship and Spiritual Formation<br>DMin, Gordon Conwell Theological Seminary

This book is beautifully written, extremely practical, and full of truth. Holly encourages us to slow down, refocus, and live with more intention. Something I think so many of us struggle with. Whether you're reading with a group or walking through it on your own, it's the kind of book that meets you exactly where you are and helps you take that next step forward.

Natasha Funderburk
Writer and Editor, Salt + Sparrow

This book is simply needed and wonderful! In *Choosing True Life*, Holly's enthusiasm for God's kind and loving nature shines through, alongside her genuine care for those who have made a decision to follow Jesus. Perfect for new followers of Jesus, but even as a seasoned Christian, one who has loved and followed Jesus for decades, I came away from reading it with my soul refreshed and my hope renewed.

Deb Gruelle, speaker, best-selling & multi-award-winning author, and grateful follower of Jesus

*Choosing True Life* is for new believers searching for a place to start! This book lays a strong foundation for a *lifeline* and *lifetime* of walking closely with Jesus. Holly makes the gospel personal, welcoming, and compelling. This is discipleship that changes lives—a must-read for all who are searching for a deeper relationship with their Savior.

Tim Koenning
Director of Missions, Amor Real Ministries

*Choosing True Life* is a rare blend of spiritual depth and everyday practicality. Holly helps readers see that transformation is not found in one dramatic moment, but in the daily decision to walk with Jesus. This is a book that will stay with you long after you close the final page.

Peggy Townes
Executive Director of Briarwood Ballet
Peru Missions Leader 2019 & 2023

*Choosing True Life* is a refreshing and deeply meaningful guide for anyone longing to move beyond the motions of everyday life and into a fuller walk with Jesus. Holly Compton gently leads readers through thirty choices that anchor the heart in Scripture and invite real transformation. Her use of Jesus' first miracle beautifully illustrates how God takes our ordinary and turns it into something rich and purposeful.

What I love most about this book is its blend of honesty, hope, and practical spiritual steps. Holly speaks to real struggles—discouragement, healing, identity—and points us back to the only One who can truly change us. This isn't self-help; it's an invitation to depend on the Savior who restores and renews.

I wholeheartedly recommend *Choosing True Life* to anyone seeking a deeper, more vibrant relationship with Christ.

Tecia Janes
Founder & Director of Choosing Him Ministries

In the pages of this book, Holly invites us into a more intentional way of following Jesus—one daily choice at a time. Her insights are grounded, practical, and full of hope. Her writing is so relatable, and her vibrant personality shines through every word. Women's groups, discipleship groups, and individuals seeking to daily encounter Jesus, as well as experience spiritual growth, will find this book to be a meaningful and encouraging resource.

Alison Lusted
Co-Founder of CrossPoint Ministries
and Certified Trauma Resolution Therapist

**This book is a gift for:**

______________________________________

**because I want you to know Who *True Life* really is.**

**From:**

______________________________________

**Date:**

______________________________________

To my husband, Alex, the most perfect gift
God ever gave me,
to my children, Eden, Elianna, and Esaias,
and to my children's children.
May you continue a legacy of choosing *True Life*.
To my mother, Cathy, whose selfless love and faith have
been my daily example.
And in loving memory of Warren McDowell,
whose friendship and encouragement will live on
through this book.

# Acknowledgments

My husband, Alex—you believed in me when I didn't have a clue how to write a book. Then you gave me everything I needed to follow through. I'm so honored to be your wife, and I love you forever. You are the living, breathing grace of God in my life.

Thank you to my children, Eden, Elianna, and Esaias, for giving Mom the grace and space to write. You have each blessed my life in incredible ways that gave every word of this book authenticity and integrity.

Thank you to Cathy Chipolone-Collins, Pastors Robert & Jennifer Walker, and all my family at The Prayer Room Church, for encouraging me and cheering me on to finish the assignment God has given me.

Thank you to all of my many beta readers and editors who provided immense feedback and encouragement and really brought out my voice. Thank you to Megan Brown for her kind guidance that made this book what it was meant to be. I could not have done this without any of you!

And finally, thank you to Nika Maples and all of my fellow Anointed Writers, hope*writers, and hope*books authors, for the right instructions, encouragement, prayers, and advice in God's perfect time for me to finally make this book a reality.

# Table of Contents

# Foreword

*Choosing True Life* is a gentle guide, a faithful companion, and a spiritual compass for every believer stepping into the breathtaking journey of following Jesus. Holly Compton has written a treasure for the global Church, distilling decades of faith and ministry into thirty transformational choices that awaken the heart, anchor the soul, and illuminate the path of true discipleship.

With clarity, compassion, and a contagious love for Jesus, Holly invites readers—from brand-new believers to seasoned followers longing for renewal—into a lifestyle shaped by daily surrender, deep trust, and courageous spiritual growth. Each chapter feels like an intimate conversation with a wise friend who has walked the narrow way and discovered its hidden joys. Her brilliant manuscript offers practical steps, biblical insight, and revelatory simplicity—perfect for personal devotion, group discipleship, and cross-cultural ministry.

As Holly leads Amor Real Ministries into nations far and near, her message carries an unmistakable authenticity. This book is not a theory. It is lived wisdom—born from missions, prayer rooms, hard-won breakthroughs, and God-encounters that mark a life fully yielded to Christ. I know you'll be thrilled to discover these 30 transformational choices!

By Dr. Brian Simmons

Lead Translator of *The Passion Translation*®,
Co-Founder of Passion & Fire Ministries, Inc.
International speaker, best-selling author,
traveler, husband, & follower of Christ

# Introduction

**(Please don't skip me!)**

There was nothing left.

No home. No job. No school. No fiancé. No plan. No joke.

It felt as if every dream I had ever cherished had met its violent end. I cried harder than I ever had before, searching desperately for a sliver of hope. And I'm happy to tell you, Hope did come...eventually.

What I didn't realize back in 2002, when everything fell apart, is the quiet misstep that sent the boulder rolling down the mountain. In my search for a true "home," I leapt toward a job that seemed perfect. I thought it was an open door from God—it led me to a potential spouse, a great church, and a life that looked beautifully on track. Looking back now, I smile at my younger self and the trail of naïve, disastrous choices I made. Ah, to be that young and certain again!

It was all fun and games until this "home" I had constructed started to collapse: first my job, then my education, and finally my relationship. In what felt like seconds, the security I had worked so hard to create was swallowed by a black hole of hurt.

In truth, my safe space had always been wherever my mom was. Her presence brought comfort no matter how heavy the day. Just hearing her voice could steady my heart through the toughest moments of college. After graduation, I tried to recreate that sense of safety—steady job, solid church, new friends, another degree program, a boyfriend. But none of it felt as safe or certain as "home." I used to tell myself, *Home is where the mom is!* Yet losing everything showed me a deeper truth: there is only one true homing signal for the heart, and His name is Jesus.

Since there are no secrets here, let me rewind.

Upon my college graduation, I was offered two jobs, one at the church I had been attending throughout college under my fatherly Pastor Dennis, who had discipled me and prayed me through four difficult years. However, because of the draw of salary and benefits, I accepted the other offer as the Administrative Assistant to the Faculty at Andover Newton Theological School in Boston (now part of Yale Divinity School). As an employee, I could take classes for free, so I enrolled in a Master of Divinity program. Because I was a student, I could live on campus in a lovely studio apartment. Life felt full—purposeful even. I met a wonderful man (let's call him Joe) at my new church, and he gave me a ring in August 2001. A month later, with my spiral wedding planner in hand, Joe and I joined the rest of the world as we watched terror unfold on September 11, 2001.

Fast forward to spring 2002. The aftershocks of 9/11 rippled deeply in our hearts—and in the Boston economy.

For so many, Joe and I included, the world felt upside down, and I still had no idea how much worse it was about to get.

One ordinary morning, the Dean of Students called me into his office, along with the HR manager—my first clue that something bad was about to happen. He assured me I had done nothing wrong, and I might've believed him, but both of their faces were beet red with anxiety. A nervous knot twisted in my stomach as I sat down. Then, as if ripping off a Band-Aid, they told me my position had been eliminated, effective immediately.

Those were words I never saw coming—sharp enough to slice through silence and set my frantic insides to upend, uptick, and upheave.

With shaky hands, I packed up my belongings, unsure how this ordinary day had soured so quickly. Then it struck me... I no longer belonged to the school. My role had vanished, my degree hung in limbo, and my housing hurtled into uncertainty. Not long after, Joe and I faced the painful truth that we had built our worlds around each other instead of around God. As my half of that world began to crumble, the ground around us gave way, and our breakup followed like an aftershock.

When I finally caught my breath, I began sifting through the rubble of my choices. *What if* I'd taken the other job I was offered? *What if* Joe and I had chosen to include God in our relationship? *What if...* But where I saw ruins, another person saw possibility. A Christian counselor gently called it a "do-over." I could start again—this time building on Christ as my rock, not on the instability of sand. That conversation undeniably marked the arrival of Hope in my life.

Maybe you're reading this and thinking about your own not-quite-right choices too. If so, take heart—there's grace for that! God uses everything, even our mistakes, to move us from one season into the next. There's nothing you've done that God can't redeem for your good and His glory.

Now, a quick confession: this is *not* a *self*-help book. I'm writing with deep compassion for you—because although we've likely never met, I've prayed for you. Yes, you. I care for you because I know what it's like to feel stuck in the aftermath of choices, to carry regret like a heavy stone. Many of us live with that weight—caught between fear of the future and the echo of the past. I've made my share of life-altering choices, each one shaping the journey that led me here—some ugly, some exquisite, but all were mine to make or mine to mistake.

So if this isn't self-help, what is it?

It's an invitation—to transformation.

What if you could break free from the past? What if you could live fully, freely, with purpose and peace? The good news is that change is not only possible—it's promised. You don't need perfection or a spotless history to begin walking in a new direction.

As I share these 30 choices that are foundational to faith, I'm inviting you to choose something radically different—a journey of walking in the ways of Jesus—not out of obligation or religious duty, but as a pathway to true, abundant life. It's about choosing love over fear, surrender over control, and grace over striving. It's a path that can help you overcome regret, conquer roadblocks and consequences of the past, and step into the future you were meant for.

God offers joy beyond imagining—here and now, and even more so in eternity. But there's one obstacle standing in the way: us. Every day we can make self-defeating choices we think are "good" on the basis of our own knowledge, current circumstances, and beliefs. We might even think they are God-informed and on the right track. However, we often confuse *belief in God* with *trusting and following Him.* The first may fill a pew once a week; the second calls us to surrender, to let go, to die to self—so we can truly live.

Beth Moore put it this way:

> There seems to be no limit on what we are willing to spend—in both time and money—on leadership training, job training, parental training, athletic training, potty training, and dog training, but "come and die" training is a harder sell. Yet it remains our only means of finding true life—not just after we shed these temporary bodies, but right here, right now. On this very earth, in this very era, on the very block where we live.[1]

If the idea of surrender (the "come and die" part) makes you nervous, that's a good sign. It means you're standing on holy ground, the very place God can do His best work. You don't need all the answers; you just need to be willing

1 Moore, Beth. *Chasing Vines: Finding Your Way to an Immensely Fruitful Life.* Tyndale Momentum, 2020.

to take the next step. This isn't about perfection—it's about openness to something greater than yourself.

As you journey through these pages, you'll reflect on, act, and practice the ways of Jesus through small, powerful choices. You'll find prayers to help you experience freedom that flows from walking in rhythm with the One who knows the way. This path requires courage—but it leads to peace, joy, and renewed purpose.

My hope and prayer are that, by the end, you'll lean deeper into God and trust His hands with your life. When you release control, you make space for God to bless you in ways you never imagined—but exactly as He intends. You may need to read and reread this book so that the choices you make remain fresh in your spirit.

Let's embark together on this divergent pathway. We will learn the art of surrender and obedience, the quiet hope of letting go. I promise you, God has our absolute best life in store. This is the path where we discover the magnificence of transformation in the same astounding way that Jesus turned *water* into *wine.*

# Part I:

# Choosing True Life is about a *Who*, Not a What

If you were born in America or even brought here as a child, you might have heard of

"The American Dream."

That's the fantasy ingrained in my country that you can grow up, get married, have 2.5 kids, buy a house with a white picket fence, a dog, a great job, and lots of money.

That's the world's definition of success: living the dream, arriving at the destination.

I'm sorry that we're not going *there.*

I'm *not* sorry because we're going somewhere better.

It's not a *place.*

It's a *Person.*

And the best part is,

*He's* been waiting for you your whole life.

*Chapter 1.*

# JESUS

If you've never met Jesus Christ, the only Son of God, I'm truly honored to introduce you to this Man who is my best Friend. I understand that for many people, the name Jesus can leave a sour taste in your mouth due to an array of cultural cues and worldly impressions. I certainly used to feel a similar way myself. I've struggled with wanting to hide from Him and with how to make Him matter to me personally. Maybe you have too. But let me assure you of one thing—He is safe. He's not a villain trying to brainwash you. He's not a dictator trying to make you behave. My friend, He is the one thing you've been looking for your whole life.

Stick with me as I lay out this journey for you that begins with Jesus and ends in the fulfillment of everything you've ever wanted. I'm not joking or exaggerating here. Jesus is the missing puzzle piece you've been searching for all along. You don't need to clean yourself up to get started. It's okay to initiate this journey just as you are, even if it's from a place of doubt—yes, we'll talk about that too. For now, it's enough to stand fully in your "maybe" because I'm confident that you'll discover the One who loves you so much that He laid down His life for *you*. He's the only One who can transform your pain and sorrow into a fresh, new life of joy-filled purpose. So let's begin.

## Choice #1 – What's In It For You?

People have loved movies since the first motion picture was shown to an audience in Paris, France, in 1895. We're easily enchanted by what I call "The Miracle Factor." We put our trust in film creators to skillfully depict an attention-grabbing, climactic adventure for one or more characters. These characters face mental, physical, emotional, or spiritual upheaval, which facilitates rapid, magnificent growth by the end—a perfect and prompt transformation before our very eyes. We watch on the edge of our seats as everything falls apart, only to be wrapped back up in a pretty and poised bow by the end.

Let me just put this out there—this book is *not* the movies.

As we well know, in real, everyday life, things don't always work out so flawlessly. Sure, the cinematic "Miracle Factor" draws us in every time. But why? Why are we so captivated by the evident grandeur of cinematic metamorphosis?

The truth is, we secretly, desperately long for the same transformation in us. A change in our everyday lives, in our current trajectory, or in our stagnant perspective. Anything to not only fill the void in our lives, but to also last so we, too, can be fully satisfied.

I think it's safe to say most of us can recognize there is an empty hole in our souls. A deep longing for something more than this world itself can provide. Augustine, a fourth-century theologian, believed there was only one path to abundance, saying to God, "You have made us for Yourself, and our hearts are restless until they find their rest in You."[2] He echoes the words of the Bible that point to the completion we seek that comes from God alone:

- ***In Mind:*** "You open your hand and satisfy the desires of every living thing." (Psalm 145:16, NIV)
- ***In Body:*** "For He satisfies the parched throat and fills the hungry appetite with what is good." (Psalm 107:9)
- ***In Spirit:*** "For I [fully] satisfy the weary soul, and I replenish every languishing and sorrowful person." (Jeremiah 31:25)

The true void within is an infinite, God-shaped hole, waiting for a fullness from the only One capable of filling it. In recognizing this, we have a choice to make. Are we going to pursue the One who can truly give us what we actually need, or will we pursue self-pleasing but temporary methods of satisfaction, like food, pleasure, power, sex, alcohol, drugs, exercise, physical beauty, money, material possessions, fame, etc.? The list goes on and on here, but none of it will ever be enough. What God offers us is more than just satisfying our physical needs; He offers what we desire most. If we have the courage to push through, just like we watch our favorite movie characters do in picturesque film phenomena, an absolute truth emerges—God is the only *true* source of fulfillment. And with that fulfillment,

2 Augustine, Saint. *Confessions*. Translated by Henry Chadwick, Oxford University Press, 1991.

He enables us to transcend who and what we are to who and what we long to become. It's only when the truth of God is embraced that our souls sigh and conclude, "That was a *good* movie."

In the Apostle Paul's letter to the Ephesians, he wrote:

> That, regarding your previous way of life, you put off your old self [completely discard your former nature], which is being corrupted through deceitful desires, and be continually renewed in the spirit of your mind [having a fresh, untarnished mental and spiritual attitude], and put on the new self [the regenerated and renewed nature], created in God's image, [godlike] in the righteousness and holiness of the truth [living in a way that expresses to God your gratitude for your salvation]. (Ephesians 4:22-24)

This is the same developmental arc we witness in movies and books. In the words of Paul, it's a renewal "in the spirit of your mind," a regeneration and an "untarnished spiritual attitude." And as that journey begins, we have a choice to make. How will we walk it out? In pursuit of the former nature and its superficial values, or in pursuit of godly values in gratitude? That, too, is laid out for us in Romans:

> And do not be conformed to this world [any longer with its superficial values and customs], but be transformed and progressively changed [as you mature spiritually] by the renewing of your mind [focusing on godly

> values and ethical attitudes], so that you may prove [for yourselves] what the will of God is, that which is good and acceptable and perfect [in His plan and purpose for you]. (Romans 12:2)

God has a purpose for each of us, and this entire book is dedicated to the choices we have to make in order to find out what that purpose is. Choices like: Are you living or dying? What are you pursuing to fill that God-shaped hole in your soul? Will you live empty or find the fulfillment you crave and satisfy your soul?

I know, these are difficult choices, ones we are all faced with every single day. If you take one thing away from this book, I pray it's an understanding that without God, life is bleak. But with God, even in the toughest storms of life, He will be with you every step of the way to lead and bring peace and give joy that surpasses all understanding. That's what's in it for *you*. I've lived both ways, and I will never go back to living only for myself again. What will you choose?

## Choice Challenge

Where do you see yourself in the journey of "The Miracle Factor"? Are you stuck at the beginning where transformation seems impossible, or at least improbable? Will you take the first step toward the renewal of your mind, body, and soul? Write down three simple ways that you can begin to implement your choice. (For example, reading the Bible for five minutes every morning, praying while you brush your teeth, or sharing three things you're thankful for in your life when you eat dinner.)

## Prayer

*God, I want to believe that You are enough to satisfy my soul. Will You show me the path to fulfillment? I choose to start trusting You today. I choose to believe You're good and You have a purpose for my life. Please help me to release my desires that are not of You and to pursue You and not the world around me. Amen.*

## Choice #2 – Life or Death?

Happiness is such an odd thing in this life. As a child of abuse, I chased hints of happiness with everything I had. What started with cigarettes and perfectionism turned into a desperate need for control and acceptance. What have you been chasing?

I don't ask this to point out your flaws. The truth is, we all hold out for hope that one day we'll find that one perfect thing to make us so happy we'll never feel the crushing weight of disappointment again. That one thing that will change *everything.* We cry out to anything we deem powerful, like God or the universe, to obtain it, and we become willing to sell our very souls for it.

The problem with striving to be happy is that it's unsustainable. Happiness is a feeling, just like anger, and chasing it leaves us rundown with nowhere solid to plant our feet. I've learned the hard way that our feelings are liars, and liars can only be stopped with the truth. So let me ask, what do you think is the biggest lie told in friend groups, classrooms, conferences, and even some churches?

"Do what makes *you happy*," right? "Do *you*."

I mean, it's written on walls, placed on bumper stickers, and jamming up our Instagram feeds. The reality is, however, that doing things that make us unhappy or frustrated or challenged is what brings growth to our character and builds a foundation of contentment. For example, exercising doesn't *feel* great, but it builds muscle and helps our bodies function better than without it.

Every choice we make carries a consequence—good or bad—for ourselves and those around us. As a young adult, I desperately wanted to choose the right things, the good things, but my own spiritual emptiness kept me from choosing a sustainable joy through Christ over happiness. Eventually I learned that it literally takes one step, one choice, one move toward God, and joy will be freely given to us by Him. We so easily crumble under poor judgment and rebellion as we function in prideful thoughts like, *I can do it on my own*, or subconscious arrogance in assuming we know better than others, which is a mindset that knows no age limit.

In my childhood, the Bible rarely made an appearance, even at our Episcopal church services, because we used the *Book of Common Prayer* in its place. In my strive for perfection and affirmation, I memorized most of it and tried to find comfort in the repetitive phrases, choruses, and prayers. I told myself, *The answers must be in here,* as I dove into yet another source that wouldn't satisfy me. I knew the words, but I didn't know how they applied to me. I wanted to attend every church service, hoping the words would fill up this emptiness I felt inside me, but they never did. So, I filled the void with cigarettes, which didn't bring me much enjoyment, so I briefly branched out to drugs and alcohol, also to no avail. I wanted to be loved, valued, and accepted, but instead, my choices only brought brokenness and bondage.

The Bible is filled with stories of people who made significantly poor choices. Some of them turned back to God for forgiveness, and others didn't. That's the blessing and curse of free will; we have the option to mess it all up. There are times when I wish I could go back and tell my teenage self to stop running from the only thing that will fill the need I had, but if I hadn't walked through all I did, I wouldn't be here with you in this moment. Since I can't go back and tell myself, I will tell you. Please don't waste any more time. There is nothing in this world that will bring the abundant blessing of true life with Jesus except a relationship with Him.

So, here's what we both need to know. In Deuteronomy 30:19-20, we read Moses' invitation to the people of Israel:

> I call heaven and earth as witnesses against you **today**, that I have set before you ***life and death, the blessing and the curse***; *therefore, you shall* ***choose life*** *in order that you may live*, you and your descendants, by loving the Lord your God, by obeying His voice, and by holding closely to Him; for He is ***your life [your good life, your abundant life, your fulfillment***] and the length of your days, that you may live in the land which the Lord promised *(swore)* to give to your fathers, to Abraham, Isaac, and Jacob. (emphasis added)

Life and death. Man, that choice feels heavy, doesn't it? I mean, we are always free to avoid the choice altogether, but avoiding it is, in turn, choosing death. Being stuck in survival mode isn't survival; it's death in waiting. For many of us, avoidance is rooted in pride and a lack of trust in God. But friend, dragging out our time in control only creates more chains of bondage. The good news is that it doesn't have to be that way. No matter how you've lived, you can make the choice right here and now to change your life for the better. You don't have to have all the answers or navigate this path alone; once you choose a life lived for God, you'll never be alone again.

Let me give you a little more backstory here about God's chosen people, known as Israel. Deuteronomy 30:19–20 occurs at the close of Moses' final message to Israel as they stand on the edge of the Promised Land (a lush and amazing home that God promised them He'd provide, the one place on earth they searched for in the desert for 40 years). Knowing he will not be going with them, Moses reminds the people of the covenant they made with God and the blessings that come from loving and obeying Him. He places before them a clear choice—life and blessing or death and loss—and urges them to "choose life" by loving God, walking in His ways, and holding fast to Him. In this passage, "life" is not just physical existence, but a life rooted in God's presence, protection, and purpose. Moses emphasizes that God Himself is the true source of life, and the future of the nation depends on their decision to remain faithful to Him.

The choice Moses presents is a **covenant choice**—a decision of loyalty, relationship, and direction. Israel was not being asked to follow God out of mere duty, but to enter into a committed relationship in which their identity, well-being, and future were tied to Him. This matters today because we also face the same foundational decision in our daily lives: to rely on God and walk in His ways, or to turn to our own understanding and live separated from

His guidance and blessing. Moses' message is clear and still true now: **Choosing God = choosing life. Turning from God = choosing death.** The call to "choose life" is ultimately an invitation to love God, trust Him, and cling to Him, recognizing that true life—purpose, hope, strength, and peace—comes not from circumstances or self-effort, but from relationship with Him.

This kind of invitation is not one you find in the everyday world around us. Society tells us we are the masters of our own fate, and perhaps there is a sliver of truth in there somewhere. We are taught from an early age how to live a self-serving existence. We learn that life is about *me, more, mine;* our focus is rudimentary. Each day God gives us the freedom to make choices. This matters because when we choose Him, not out of force or obligation, it becomes a place where a meaningful relationship can grow.

In the book of Joshua, Joshua makes a declaration to Israel after God renewed His covenant with them in the Promised Land, as we just discussed. He says, "Choose for yourselves this day whom you will serve" (Joshua 24:15). For Israel, this was about moving past their fears and declaring God as their Lord above all. Joshua uses the word *serve* here. To serve someone, we must have a master. To have a master, we must be wholeheartedly devoted to that master. In biblical times, this notion of having a master was not nearly as scary as it may seem to you right now; people would choose to sit as students beneath a teacher whom they would address and regard as their master. So stick with me; having a master isn't as harsh as it sounds, I promise.

Throughout the Old Testament, we watch Israel struggle in this awful cycle of wrath and surrender as they waver between idols and God. While it might not be a statue or an actual person, we all worship a master, giving away pieces of ourselves, until our thoughts are consumed by it. Lysa TerKeurst writes, "What we fix our attention, heart, and mind on is what we'll worship. What we worship becomes magnified. And what is magnified will consume us and perpetuate more and more worship."[3] In other words, we all have true devotion to a master to whom we're willing to abandon our souls—which includes our mind, will, and emotions—and fully surrender our right to choose our own path.

So the question remains, who will our master be? Matthew 6:24 says:

> No one can serve two masters; for either he will hate the one and love the other, or he will be devoted to the one and despise the other. You cannot serve God and mammon [money, possessions, fame, status, or whatever is valued more than the Lord].

This is our reminder to daily ask ourselves: Who is the master of my heart? Whatever came to your mind first is the thing, or idol, that you're serving. Now, I'm not saying that what came to mind isn't warranted because there are many options that occupy our daily thoughts. Loving my husband brings me immense joy. My children make me smile from ear to ear. Money enables us to live, eat, have shelter, etc. Food is delicious and nutritious. Satisfied

---

3 TerKeurst, Lysa. *Made to Crave Devotional.* Thomas Nelson, 2011.

tummies feel good. The problem is, even good things can turn into idols when we place them higher than God in our hearts. When we put our faith and trust in something that cannot fill the God-sized hole within us, we lose out on the kind of life that God offers.

I understand the struggle of idols, as I've made many throughout my life. Food became a major one in my adolescence, leaving me sixty-five pounds overweight by the time I was fourteen. Being overweight made me feel ashamed and imperfect (and the bullying over the years didn't help), so I did what I thought best and became anorexic overnight. Disgusted by my journey up to that point, I made a choice to stop and go the opposite direction the very next day. I rapidly lost the weight in two months, and yet no one questioned it. Maybe those around me were just happy I *looked* healthier. Isn't that how it works? With idols, a person can look healthy, and yet their soul is suffocating with decay, rotting from the inside out, just like a teen with anorexia.

At the time, I felt proud of my choices because they produced the results I had so longed for: praise for losing the weight, the attention and affection of boys/men, the end of the bullying and the shame. Sadly, I didn't understand the damage that was happening to my body and soul. It took years for me to acknowledge the fact that there are only two choices in this life: serve ourselves or serve God. And treating my body like garbage was definitely not the latter.

Choosing to be our own master or god is idolatry, too, which is repeatedly explored in the Bible as a sin. Since the fall of Adam and Eve in the Garden of Eden, we are all born with the fleshly desire to control everything in our lives, to be captain of our own ship. But here's the thing to understand: you can believe in God and still serve yourself. Let me say that one more time so it can really sink in. We can acknowledge who God is and still focus on ourselves. Don't worry, there's still hope because even when we do this, we always have the choice to change and begin to choose God more than ourselves. But frankly, the more we choose self over God, the more deadly the result. This is echoed throughout Scripture, which tells us, "For the wages of sin is death" (Romans 6:23). I know this seems harsh, but it is serious business. We pay for our self-serving posture with earthly lives weighed down by rigid, heavy chains on our souls, plus an eternal life of torment because we will be separated from God and everything good.

Sadly, the unfortunate question is, when we are forced to face the consequences of our own actions, who do we blame? I struggled with this in my early life as a Christian. I blamed God above anything or anyone else. I saw Him as mean and self-serving, and I felt as if my current hardship was His punishment for how I lived. What I didn't understand was how my self-defeating actions were to blame, not God.

As I shared above, Deuteronomy 30:19-20 tells us that "death" is the equivalent of a "curse." The biblical definition of a curse is "a pronouncement of judgment or misfortune, often due to disobedience of God's commands." The consequences—or curses—that we endure are a direct result of our problematic actions which staunchly defy the standards of God. Please don't mistake this, because when awful things happen in this world or in our lives, we tend to worry if God caused it or if it is a punishment of some sort, but that is not the case. When our choices bring forth hardship, that's on us. When our loved one gets cancer or a child dies, that is the direct result of evil in this world. God does not cause horrific things to happen, but He can take that pain and bring forth something beautiful that gives glory to Him and hope to us.

On the other hand, the definition of "blessing" is "God's favor and protection." Here, life is covered and satisfied despite our circumstances or grief. It's the opportunity to live through His strength, wisdom, and power in the best of times and the worst of times. It's being saturated with God's favor and love and being protected by God's own hand. This is what joy looks like. It's sustainable by God, provided abundantly, and filtered through our trust and faith–and it's available to all who **believe in Him**.

Before we end our time together today, I want to ask you if there is an elephant in the room here. Trust me, there is no judgment if so. I'm wondering if you might have a few foundational questions, such as: What if I struggle with believing that God exists? And if He does exist, is He good? Especially if He is apparently telling us that if we don't choose *Him*, we'll die!

These are questions I understand wholeheartedly because I asked them frequently throughout my teen years. The first thing I want you to know is that these questions are normal. God is not disappointed or irritated with you when or if you ask them. The first thing to address is the why of it all: why do we struggle to believe and then again to surrender?

The basic reality is, we can't *see* God. I can be very logical at times, and until age 16, I believed in what I could see. But, here's the thing. I can't see love. I can only see how someone deeply cares for another in their words, actions, and attitudes. I can't see the wind. But I can certainly feel it flying in my face, tossing around my hair, or blowing objects around in a hurricane. Both love and wind have the capacity to embrace us—wind in the physical realm and love in the spiritual. Love and wind can also destroy. If love is suddenly removed, the heart-bending betrayal must be forgiven or the emotionally painful loss must be grieved. If wind picks up speed, tornadoes can wreak havoc for miles on end. While we can't see love or wind with our eyes, their effects are undeniable.

When I was 16, I said a simple prayer, "God, if You're real, please show me." I had so many questions at the time, and God provided knowledgeable believers who did their best to answer them until my heart was ready to take the leap of faith. That leap of faith brought God out into the light so I *could* see Him, living in the hearts of my new friends and giving life to the world. Amid that scary leap, I found the pathway to True Life. And along that path, He showed me His good, kind, loving nature through the promises He made to me and His faithfulness to fulfill them.

I had one other big problem, however. Believing in God, embracing Him as my pathway to True Life, didn't immediately mean I was ready to live *His* way. I was a control freak! (Can you relate?) I still wanted to live *my* way, do things He didn't want me to do, and exist in my state of comfort. Surrender? Nope, not an option (for another few years, anyway).

Elizabeth Gilbert once posted on Instagram, "You are afraid of surrender because you don't want to lose control. But you never had control; all you had was anxiety."[4] Because we don't know what the future holds, whether through our own choices or in surrender to an unfamiliar God, it can leave us riddled with fear and anxiety. We go about our lives trying to build a foundation on whatever we perceive will give us the most power and control, but we are remiss to find full satisfaction in this pursuit.

Timothy Keller writes, "Spiritual darkness—turning away from God, the true light, and making anything more important than him—leads invariably from disorientation to disintegration."[5] Keller is drawing us a picture of death—while we're still living on this earth. When we turn away from the light of God, we end up in a disorienting darkness. Have you ever been in an unfamiliar room where it's so dark you can't see your hand in front of your face? You have no light to show you the way out. When we can't find our way out of our internal darkness, those pesky "curses" cause a myriad of hardships, which break us down and chip away at the person God created us to be. Our spirits become disoriented when we do not have a Rock (God) to stand on, and slowly everything that makes us who we are begins to fall away–or disintegrate—until nothing is left. Without that Rock, we fall victim to the sinking sand until it swallows us whole. That's spiritual death.

4 Gilbert, Elizabeth [@elizabeth_gilbert_writer]. *Instagram*, 12 July 2020, https://www.instagram.com/p/CCizu4cB7CU/.

5 Keller, Timothy. *King's Cross: The Gospel of Mark*. Dutton, 2011.

The hope in all this is that God promises to bring blessing to those who love and follow Him, to be the goodness and fulfillment we're searching for, and to be our protector. He reminds us that our man-made foundations are as sturdy as the sand, easily displaced and blown about, unable to support or hold anything steady: Jesus said, "And everyone who hears these words of Mine and does not do them, will be like a foolish (stupid) man who built his house on the sand" (Matthew 7:26). I know that's exactly how the foundation I built for myself in 2002 felt; what about you?

I have no idea how you started to read this book or why, but if you find yourself standing at a crossroads today and have never understood the choices before you, then I pray today is *the* day to choose life, choose blessing, and leave the curse of death behind you. Choose God and surrender your life to His hands.

## Choice Challenge

Do you believe you have it all together, or do you recognize your need for God? Will you choose to pursue fulfillment in the world, or will you devote yourself to the one true God who leads to life? True Life, or ultimately, death. The blessings, or the curse. You choose. Then, write a letter to God, just like you would send an email to a friend, and tell Him *why*. He can't wait to hear from you!

## Prayer

*God, I'm not sure if You're real or if You're good, but if You are, please show Yourself to me. Give me the strength to choose You instead of my own self-worship. Help me surrender it all to You so that I might choose life instead of death. Help me take this leap of faith, God. I confess that I can't do it on my own. Amen.*

## Choice #3 – Who is Your Champion?

Choosing life over death is just the beginning of God's work in our lives. It's simply the starting line of discovering who we were always meant to be. God didn't create any of us to be depressed and overwhelmed with anxiety. In my life, I struggled deeply with depression. Many days, I couldn't get out of bed, let alone function well as a wife and mother. And in 2016, He answered my long-awaited prayers and healed me from depression, which I will tell you more about later. However, it would be reckless of me to allow you to believe God will answer every prayer with a yes. He uses hardship to teach us how to depend firmly on Him. Believe it or not, we need Him, even on a simple grocery store trip.

To say that we "need" Him doesn't really do justice to the messiness our lives can contain without Him. When you take into account our fragile humanity, the sinking sand beneath our feet, our spiritual darkness, and our self-idolatry, we can quickly admit that left to our own devices, we are hardly qualified to make sense of the chaos or piece back together the shambles of our lives that we've produced. We need *help*. Not just any help, not just a crutch—we need a *Champion*. The definition of "champion" is "an ardent defender of a cause or person." We cannot save ourselves, defend ourselves, or create significant change in our lives without this Champion. So we must stay close to this Champion to the best of our ability.

Remember that old champion-less mindset, "I can do this on my own," that we carelessly believe at times? The truth is that no matter how great, independent, or powerful we think we are, we're still just *water*. Let me explain.

Humans need water to survive. We can't go more than three days without it, or we'll die from dehydration.[6] Our brain and heart together are made up of 73% water, and our lungs alone are made up of 83% water.[7] According to the USGS Water Science School, Earth's surface is made up of 71% of... you guessed it, water.[8] Interesting, right?

Water is the basis of all life. It's essential for our bodies and this planet to survive. It is one hundred percent necessary for all living things, which is why I call it the "essential life." Water has some unique qualities; for example, it can boil and turn from a liquid to a gas, or it can freeze and become a solid. Water can also act with tremendous force. It can pull you into the ocean by an undertow. It can erode rock bit by bit. Water can destroy anything in its path and even bring forth death. It holds so many capabilities, both essentially helpful and harmful.

Although water is the best thing we can drink, I can't help but think about how bored I might feel drinking only water because water is, well, boring. Oh yeah, I said what I said. I enjoy a little flavoring of my choice or a good unsweet

---

6 "Living Without Water," *Svalbardi*, https://svalbardi.com/blogs/water/living-without#:~:text=The%20general%20consensus%20is%20that. Accessed April 9, 2022

7 Mitchell, H.H., et al. *The Chemical Composition of the Adult Human Body and its Bearing on the Biochemistry of Growth.* Division of Animal Nutrition and Departments of Physiology and Animal Husbandry, University of Illinois, Urbana, 15 Feb. 1945, https://bionumbers.hms.harvard.edu/files/625.full.pdf. Accessed 9 Apr. 2022.

8 U.S. Geological Survey. "How Much Water Is There on Earth?" *USGS Water Science School*, U.S. Geological Survey, n.d., https://www.usgs.gov/water-science-school/science/how-much-water-there-earth#:~:text=About%2071%20percent%20of%20the. Accessed 9 Apr. 2022.

tea like we do here in the South, or even a can of Coke (soda or pop for the rest of you). Water alone has no flavor, no color—no grand, celebratory use.

You might be wondering, what's my point here?

Well, what happens when we add God—*the* Champion of all champions—into our lives?

Have you ever heard the ageless story of the miracle of turning *water* into *wine*? It is my absolute favorite biblical story of transformation. Only in God's world does water have the ability to change instantly into wine. In that one moment, the "essential life" becomes what I call the "celebratory life."

At a wedding feast in biblical times, where this story takes place, it was customary for most families to serve the best wine first so it could be fully enjoyed while everyone was sober (and to establish family social status), and then the cheaper wine would be served next. But in this particular story, the worst thing has happened, and they've run completely out of wine. To serve watered-down wine or even worse, water alone, would have humiliated and disgraced this family. So Mary offers a solution and begs her son Jesus to do something to help their friends.

Performing this miracle not only proved God's intimate and hands-on involvement but also His delicate and personalized provision. Water, the most basic of elements at a meal, was miraculously turned into wine, which represented a celebration at its greatest moment.

How does all this apply to us? Well, we have another choice to make. We can stay just water, with no hope of change, becoming stagnant, lifeless, even undrinkable. We can choose to be half-in, like watered-down wine, where we allow some personal change but dilute it with our sin, our lack of vulnerability, and our lack of true surrender to Christ. Or, we can choose to allow Jesus to fully and miraculously transform us. By changing the foundational properties that once left us tasteless, Jesus can create something so much more beautiful and unique.

Let me give you a little peek into the background. Making wine begins by growing quality grapes on strong vines. The process of winemaking has five generalized steps, including harvesting at the right time, crushing the fruit, fermentation, blending, and bottling. The second step, crushing, is the repeated procedure whereby the pressing of the grapes and breaking of the skins set free the contents of the fruit, also known as the pulp, or "must." The crushing of the grapes feels like such a brutal thing, but it's necessary to extract the flavors well. Then the time from harvest to actual drinking can vary from a few months to over twenty years for wine of solid taste and structure.

Clearly, a great deal of time and effort goes into winemaking. The quality of the grapes is of the utmost importance. So the grapes must start by coming from a quality vine, then must be picked at just the right time for maximum flavor—it is what sets good wine apart.

Just like those grapes, life has a tendency to crush everyone. You'd be hard-pressed (pun intended) to find a single person on this planet who hasn't endured something they thought would crush them beyond repair. Trials come to everybody. They don't discriminate based on gender, race, dialect, or what street you live on. No amount of money in your bank account can save you from difficulties. The good news is we have the freedom to choose how to handle each trial as they come. Do we fight the situation and try to figure out these challenges on our own? Or do we submit ourselves to God's process, putting ourselves in the hands of our Champion vintner, so that we can become a cherished wine?

After the crushing of the grapes, most vineyards wait a minimum of seven years before the grapes are established enough to be fermented well. Secondly, the fermentation process itself is *slow*. The grape juice must sit in barrels for years, and the biggest kicker is that the longer the fermentation, the better the wine. So the winemaker can't be in a hurry. To make wine is a commitment of nurturing and consistency. Thankfully, our God is both of those things—merciful and faithful—now and forever. He doesn't sway in His stance or get distracted, but He is attentive and careful to proceed in just the right way at just the right time, always. In other words, our Champion happens to see all and know all and has perfect timing. He also doesn't produce anything but the best.

Just being water might feel like a good place for some who are content with the life they are living. It might seem easy, uncomplicated, flowing without adversity, comfortable, and familiar. Changing might feel terrifying and even catastrophic to you or those around you. But ask yourself, is it possible there might be more to this life than complacency and relentless emptiness?

The biblical story in the book of John describing this *water*-to-*wine* transformation says,

> And when the headwaiter tasted the water which had turned into wine, not knowing where it came from (though the servants who had drawn the water knew) he called the bridegroom, and said to him, "Everyone else serves his best wine first, and when people have drunk freely, then he serves that which is not so good; but you have kept back the good wine until now." (John 2:9-10)

This extravagant miracle wasn't just about plain old, end-of-the-celebration wine. The water became the *best* wine, which surpassed even the greatness of its predecessor at this wedding feast. So when we allow the Lord to change us from *water* to *wine*, there may be times in the midst of it that feel uncomfortable, intimidating, even frightening, or like nothing is happening. In those times, He is purposely but also gently allowing you to simmer—because it's in the fermentation process that juice is transformed into the best, celebratory wine to be poured out and shared.

So I urge you to stop thinking you have it all under control by yourself, because God offers us hope that the best wine is yet to come. Jesus said:

> I am the Vine, you are the branches. When you're joined with me and I with you, the relation intimate and organic, the harvest is sure to be abundant. Separated, you can't produce a thing. Anyone who separates from me is deadwood, gathered up and thrown

> on the bonfire. But if you make yourselves at home with me and my words are at home in you, you can be sure that whatever you ask will be listened to and acted upon. This is how my Father shows who he is—when you produce grapes, when you mature as my disciples. (John 15:5-8, MSG)

As our grapes mature on the Vine, their quality is ensured by our heavenly Father, our Caretaker, our Friend, our Champion. We must stay connected to the Vine, having an "intimate and organic" individualized relationship that is founded in prayer. Separate, we cannot produce any grapes—we stay bland, unchanged—*just water.*

This is the major step we need to take in order to have the intimacy with God we not only need, but also crave.

*We need The Healer. The Champion.* These are not characteristics you find in the ordinary person or something you come across on a daily basis, either. In fact, there has only ever been one Champion of True Love. Spoiler alert, it's *not us.*

The Bible says this: "There is no one who always does what is right, no, not even one! There is no one...who seeks after God alone. All have deliberately wandered from God's ways" (Romans 3:10b-12a, TPT).

Long ago, when Adam and Eve lived in the Garden of Eden, they disobeyed God by eating the forbidden fruit. Before you raise a fist to them, just know that we all would do the same thing if given the opportunity. How could we say no to becoming *like God*? None of us would choose obedience to God over ourselves in every situation for eternity. We would be led astray by our own desires, our need for comfort, and our pride in hopes of satisfying the God-shaped void we all carry within. And that, my friend, is sin.

The Bible describes God as holy, which means He is incapable of sin and is therefore pure. After Adam and Eve sinned, God cast them out of His presence because they rejected His authority and holy nature by choosing to disregard His commands. And just like in the Garden of Eden, sin forever separates us from God, and the only way to be in good standing with Him is through a blood sacrifice to pay for that sin. Timothy Keller writes,

> When the Bible talks about sin it is not just referring to the bad things we do. It's not just lying or lust or whatever the case may be—it is ignoring God in the world he has made; it's rebelling against him by living without reference to him. It's saying, "I will decide exactly how I live my life." And Jesus says that is our main problem.[9]

Because of sin, the world can't know God the way Adam and Eve did before they sinned. People can't go to Him and be accepted by Him because we are inherently impure and tarnished by our wickedness. The hard truth is, we don't deserve healing. We don't deserve His love. We don't deserve Him as a Champion and cannot earn our way back into His presence. Thankfully, God loves us so much that He provided a way back to Him:

9 Keller, Timothy. *Jesus the King: Understanding the Life and Death of the Son of God.* Penguin Books, 2013.

> In this is love, not that we loved God, but that ***He loved us*** and sent His Son to be the propitiation [that is, the atoning sacrifice, and the satisfying offering] for our sins [fulfilling God's requirement for justice against sin and placating His wrath]. (1 John 4:10, emphasis added)

What John was saying is that God took human form in the person of Jesus Christ, who, innocent of any sin, was crucified, buried, and resurrected on the third day. In doing so, Jesus fulfilled more than 300 prophecies found in the Old Testament, proving who He was and the reason He came. He paid the price with His life on the cross because He loves ***you*** so very much! ***You*** are very special to Him. God the Father couldn't stand to be separated from ***you***, so He sent His unique Son, Jesus, to be the bridge between you and Him. God wants you back in a perfect, forever connection. Jesus made the way back to the Father open and available through His death and resurrection. Speaking to His disciples, "Jesus said to him, 'I am the [only] Way [to God] and the [real] Truth and the ***[real] Life***; no one comes to the Father but through Me'" (John 14:6, emphasis added). He didn't claim to simply be a guide or an example; He claimed exclusively to be the only way to know God and embody His full truth.

***This*** is the only choice that matters. ***This*** is the choice that defines who *you* are and who will be *your master*. Jesus alone is ***real Life***. He alone is the Champion of True Love. Today, here and now, you have the freedom to choose who you will serve:

> Therefore there is now no condemnation [no guilty verdict, no punishment] for those who are in Christ Jesus [who believe in Him as personal ***Lord and Savior***]. For the law of the ***Spirit of life*** [which is] in Christ Jesus [the law of our new being] has ***set you free*** from the law of sin and of death. (Romans 8:1-2, emphasis added)

***You*** can be set free, too! Believing is the choice that unlocks the door that leads from death into life. However, believing means so much more than you think:

> Jesus said to her, "I am the Resurrection and the Life. Whoever ***believes in (adheres to, trusts in, relies on)*** Me [as Savior] will live even if he dies; and everyone who lives and believes in Me [as Savior] will never die." (John 11:25-26, emphasis added)

Believing means we cling to Jesus in two ways: as our Savior *and* our Lord. First, we trust in Jesus to save us from death, and second, we adhere to, or submit to, Jesus as our master, the One to whom we abandon ourselves and serve, in order to choose Life. Heaven is a real place. Jesus is not only the Way to get there, but He is also the Life we are dreaming of, both now and in eternity—that's the gospel, or the "good news," as it's often referred to. Keller explains that "the gospel is that God connects to you not on the basis of what you've done (or haven't done) but on the basis of what Jesus has done, in history, for you. And that makes it absolutely different from every other religion or philosophy."[10]

---

10 Keller, *Jesus the King*.

We can't earn our way to heaven as a "good person." We will never clean ourselves up enough to be seen as pure on our own. We don't have to worry about our current sins before we come to Jesus. When we reach out and accept Him into our hearts and our lives, His life sacrificed on the cross wipes our slate clean of all the things we've done wrong, haven't done, or will ever do. This is how the transformation we long for begins. Run to Him now and never let Him go.

## Choice Challenge

Jesus longs to be ***your*** Champion of True Love, if you will let Him. Will you choose to believe this plain and simple truth? Will you ask Jesus to be your Champion and walk forward with Him in intimacy? I like to think of "intimacy" as "in-to-me-see." Write down and invite Him into three areas of your life that you want to let Him see and heal. (Such as your past, your marriage, or your relationship with your parents.)

## Prayer

*Jesus, I believe in You, and I ask You to come into my heart. I confess that I am a sinner. Forgive me for all my sins, and set me free from death. Be my Lord and Savior, my Champion of True Love. I choose Life over death today. Please come into my life and change me from water into wine! In Your name I pray, Amen.*

Chapter 2.

# LORD

The word "Lord" refers to someone or something having power, authority, or influence over another. As we have discussed, this is how we relate to Jesus. He's not a dictator to whom we are enslaved, but He's a loving friend who actually knows us better than we know ourselves. And if we let Him, He will guide us along the perfect path that leads to successful fulfillment of our true purpose.

Just to clarify further, His position of authority isn't the nag-and-drag kind. He won't demand your allegiance, but when you freely offer it, He honors your choice and sacrifice and begins to show you His overall plan. As you begin to talk to Him, He'll respond through His written Word, the Bible, and directly to your heart.

A big question so many have is, "How do I know if it's God talking to me or if it's my own thoughts?" It's a great question, and it's one so many Christians, young and old, struggle with. We'll address that a little later, but for now, just know God is always talking to us in a variety of ways.

Before I really knew Jesus as my Lord, I didn't know transformation was my ultimate desire, but deep down, I craved a way out of a lonely and painful self-centeredness (the *water* life) to a hopeful and purposeful love-centeredness (the *wine* life). Now that you know your Champion, don't worry. He'll show you that, too, one surrendered step at a time.

## Choice #4 – Self or Surrender?

I've heard of friends who receive a single word from God in prayer at the beginning of the calendar year that He wants them to focus on all year long. I have never been one to dwell on anything, let alone for an entire year! But to my surprise, in 2021, for the first time, the Lord told me "renew" was to be *my* word. As I prayed about it, I felt the Lord say to my spirit, "I want to renew you completely this year, but you must first surrender." He reminded me of the "Surrender" necklace I had been given nearly twenty years earlier. It's an outline of a person on their knees with their hands up, and it came with this incredible poem attached to it:

This symbol represents the
beauty of brokenness.
Humbled heart, broken self
I lay my will upon Your shelf
wanting, longing to be filled
with Your Spirit, with Your will
take away the things that bind
as Your Word renews my mind
in Your hands I want to stay
willing, soft, moldable clay[11]

11 ©2003 Remember Me Jewelry

God asked me to wear it every day for a year to remind myself of the meaning and the method of surrender.

A biblical view of surrender is as the relinquishing of our own will, desires, and plans in exchange for those of God. The next step is to then submit to His will instead. This sounds much scarier than it is. Romans 8:15 says, "For you have not received a spirit of *slavery* leading again to fear [of God's judgment], but you have received the Spirit of adoption as *sons* [the Spirit producing sonship] by which we [joyfully] cry, 'Abba! Father!'" (emphasis added). God chose us to be His children, not His servants. I promise you, God isn't a dictator and would never insist upon your slavery. That's not the goal.

God's goal is trust. He wants to really be known by you so you may know Him as a loving Father. I realize that by saying that, you might have an earthly father who might not have been so loving. Trust me when I say, I understand. I've lived that reality too. But for argument's sake, just try and go with me here. God is perfect. He's without character flaws, without a negative, demeaning, or controlling spirit. God is love. Unconditional love. Your earthly father can never live up to God's perfect love for you, even if he was kind and caring towards you.

God is the perfect example for human fathers to follow. Unfortunately, not all do. And sometimes knowing that can leave us questioning why God would give us the commandment to honor our parents. There is a similar process between honor and surrender. To honor someone, we put our whole trust in them—submitting to their authority, courageously deciding to obey their wishes, releasing personal control, and willingly being guided by their wisdom and provision.

This can feel like a wild notion if you've grown up in an environment where you couldn't trust your parents or your family in general. Maybe you were left on your own to fend for yourself and no one has ever been there for you. Those are valid issues that I understand. The good part is that no matter what our earthly parents do or don't do, God fills in the blanks perfectly when we choose to honor Him. He will never misstep or let you down, even when it's easy to feel otherwise.

Surrendering to Him is a choice to trust in Him to carry you through even when things are unclear or difficult. It's not just about giving up control to be dominated. It's coming with respect and honor to a perfect God who desires you to live freely in and through Him, and walking in obedience to Him is the evidence of surrender.

Throughout the thirty plus years I've been a Christian, I've come back many times to psychologist and author David Benner's interpretation of surrender. He says:

> The English word *surrender* carries the implication of putting one's full weight on someone or something. It involves letting go—a release of effort, tension, and fear. And it involves trust. One cannot let go of self-dependence and transfer dependence to someone else without trust. Floating is a good illustration of this, because you cannot float until you let go.[12]

---

12 Benner, David G. *Surrender to Love: Discovering the Heart of Christian Spirituality*. InterVarsity Press, 2015.

If you've recently started walking with the Lord, choosing to trust Him may not be immediately easy. Throughout my own walk and various seasons, God has proven His faithfulness over and over. Trusting Him truly gets easier as time goes on; He is a very good Father who has been faithful to care for His followers for thousands of years. The Bible tells story after story of that faithfulness which helps increase our trust in the Lord, especially if we don't have any frame of reference for ourselves yet. We are to draw courage from these stories in order to trust God to do what He promises to do for all those who honor Him: He will unswervingly save, heal, lead, provide, and bless.

One of my favorite stories of God's faithfulness in my life begins in a strange place...a car accident! In October 2005, a coworker and I headed to a restaurant on our lunch break. As we idled at a stoplight, another car suddenly rear-ended me. My neck whipped back very hard as the car jolted us both around like rag dolls. At that exact moment, my coworker looked at me and said, "Oh, God's got good plans in store for you!"

*Huh?! What a strange thing for her to say right now,* I thought. But as life unfolded over the next two years, I began to see just how right she was. Now, unfortunately, I had a herniated disc in my neck from the accident, which required steroid injections, physical therapy, and time away from work. However, God is able to work everything out for good because I have surrendered my life to Him. Nothing that happens in our lives is wasted, and I certainly don't believe in coincidence!

In the summer of 2006, my husband, Alex, and I prepared to move to Peru as missionaries. Our tasks included raising $10,000 as seed money to establish our home and ministry in Peru. We also needed to recruit monthly financial supporters to sustain us on the mission field and pay off as much of our debt as possible. Each of these tasks seemed an insurmountable challenge, and yet we knew that God had indeed called us to do so.

Well, one year after my car accident, I settled with the other driver's insurance company for an amount that literally paid off *all* our outstanding debt with one check for $16,000. That amount was no coincidence. My coworker had been right all along—God had good plans in store for us. Trust me when I say, nothing, not even the wreckage you may be facing right now in your own life, will go to waste in God's hands. After that, things seemed to quickly click into place as we raised the other $10,000 and gained financial supporters, as required. There is no doubt in my mind that God came through faithfully.

This story always comes to mind when finances are ever a concern. God has always provided for us. For that and countless more reasons, I choose to daily place my trust in Him. I fully trust that if you don't have stories similar to this yet, you will soon, and they will quickly become the place you remember on those days where faith seems impossible.

Romans 12:1 (TPT) says, "Beloved friends, what should be our proper response to God's marvelous mercies? To surrender yourselves to God to be his sacred, living sacrifices. And live in holiness, experiencing all that delights his heart.

For this becomes your genuine expression of worship." God's gift of His Son Jesus, His goodness to restore, heal, and provide—these are His marvelous mercies that are new to us every day. So He asks us, every day, to surrender all that we are to Him who is trustworthy, doing the things that delight His heart; therein lies true worship, a self-abandoning submission to His authority. And it is from that place of submission that God begins to work in us.

What I didn't expect in 2021 was that God's definition of "renew" meant a full-life overhaul. Because I surrendered to His plan that year, God renewed my dreams (moving to Houston, writing a book, fulfilling my destiny), He renewed my vision (a new church, new ministry opportunities), He renewed my surroundings (new state, new home, new neighborhood, new neighbors, new community, new schools for my children), and He fully renewed my faith in Him as a *big* and beyond-good Father who is capable of far more than I ever thought possible.

As grateful as I am for all I just listed, what I'm most grateful for is the renewal of my mind so that I can live the way He wants me to live and receive all the blessings He has in store for me. And to think, it all started with my personal surrender to Jesus, and it can start right here with yours if you so choose:

- ***Surrender as a disciple:*** "Jesus said to all of his followers, 'If you truly desire to be my disciple, you must disown your life completely, embrace my "cross" as your own, and *surrender* to my ways.'" (Luke 9:23, TPT, emphasis added)

- ***Surrender to discover True Life:*** "Those who cling to their lives will give up true life. But those who let go of their lives for my sake and *surrender* it all to me will discover **true life**!" (Matthew 10:39, TPT, emphasis added)
- ***Surrender for prosperity and honor:*** "Laying your life down in tender *surrender* before the Lord will bring **life**, prosperity, and honor as your reward." (Proverbs 22:4, TPT, emphasis added)

I do feel it's my obligation to warn you here. Staying on the fence, straddling the half-in, half-out method of surrender, is a difficult place to remain. Having one foot in the old nature and one foot in the new is like trying to serve two gods: you and Him, and maybe you're experiencing this type of wrestling with Him in your life. Yeah, I've been there too. When I look back now at the times I squared off with God, I realize how much time I wasted thinking I knew better than Him. The truth is, tender surrender is an act of love, an act of obedience, and an act of faith.

If we seek the outcome of "life, prosperity, and honor," we must choose to honor the appropriate Authority. Dr. Tony Evans wrote: "The whole Trinity is involved in speaking to any believer who prioritizes obedience—obedience that is motivated by love for the Lord... Coming near, loving to obey Him, invites the intimacy of hearing His voice."[13] Having an intimate relationship with God is where we find our sense of belonging, where we find our own true identity, where our dreams are constantly reborn and fulfilled. This is where we

13 Shirer, Priscilla. *Discerning the Voice of God.* LifeWay Church Resources, 2017.

learn that God will never define us by our past, He does not see us for our failures, He doesn't even measure us based on our strengths. He only sees us as someone He loves and wants to be close to, which is why He continuously draws us to Himself and speaks when we're ready to listen.

At the beginning of 2022, I asked the Lord if He was going to give me another word for the year. He said, "No, 'surrender' is still your word, but this time it's not about you. It's about the generations to come." Sometimes we must realize that the world does not revolve around us or our own families; sometimes we just need to surrender because God has a much bigger plan.

## Choice Challenge

Who is your true Authority? Who would you like it to be? With all the promises that God makes to us in the Bible, you can be sure God is a safe bet. Will you trust Him enough to submit to His authority in your life? Will you surrender yourself as your act of pure worship? Write down three tangible, sacrificial ways you can submit to His authority in your day-to-day life. (Possible ways could include giving Him more time to speak to you through the Bible and prayer, or giving up certain books or movies that would not be pleasing to Him.)

## Prayer

*Dear Father, I choose now to lay my life down at Your feet and surrender. Please take my life and exchange it for the cross of Jesus. Bring me into an intimate relationship with You, that I might leave behind my old ways and embrace Yours. Bring life and prosperity to my family and me. In Jesus' name, Amen.*

## Choice #5 – Where is Your Home?

Your journey of faith may just be beginning, or perhaps you have been on this heart path for some time. Regardless, we all must make the long journey *home* to heaven. Heaven, of course, is our ultimate destination, but for the meantime, we do have a temporary home on this earth. What is *home* for you? Is it a place? A person? The word has so many possible connotations and certainly differs for every person. For me, years ago, I discovered in prayer that my true home is "where He holds my heart." Since God has my heart no matter where I am physically, I didn't put much effort into decorating the apartments or houses we have had in our married life.

That is, until now. As I first wrote this chapter, we had been living in Houston for only a few months. God encouraged me to decorate this particular house and truly make it my own, while He continues to prepare my heavenly home. The reason I felt so at home in Houston in general had very much to do with writing this book, one of many ways I am living out God's purpose for my life based on my dreams, gifts, and talents. He has told me that some of my old dreams and old promises He made to me many years ago, most of which I had long forgotten, He would revive in Houston. And indeed, He did.

While we have enjoyed these four years in Houston, our family is returning to Atlanta, where our children were born, where we became a family, and where all three of our children welcomed the Lord into their hearts. For them, Atlanta is home, our church there is their spiritual home, and it is there that they found the Lord to be their ultimate home.

The Bible actually has a lot to say about what our homes are supposed to be on this side of heaven:

- ***A Place of Godly Wisdom***: "Through [skillful and godly] wisdom a house [a life, a home, a family] is built, and by understanding it is established [on a sound and good foundation], and by knowledge its rooms are filled with all precious and pleasant riches" (Proverbs 24:3-4).
- ***A Place of Peace and Rest***: "Then my people will live in a peaceful surrounding, and in secure dwellings and in undisturbed resting places" (Isaiah 32:18).
- ***A Place of Blessing and Welcome***: "Whatever house you enter, first say, 'Peace [that is, a blessing of well-being and prosperity, the favor of God] to this house'" (Luke 10:5).
- ***A Place of Integrity***: "The curse of the Lord is on the house of the wicked, but He blesses the home of the just and righteous" (Proverbs 3:33).
- ***A Place Built by God Himself***: "For [of course] every house is built and furnished by someone, but the Builder of all things and the Furnisher [of the entire equipment of all things] is God" (Hebrews 3:4, AMPC).

None of our homes are going to be perfect; we are imperfect people. But we are called to create homes—both physically and spiritually—that are surrendered to Jesus as Lord, and with that, He enables us to create a safe haven that provides comfort and peace to those who reside within, a place to escape the chaos of this world, a place that's even a foretaste of heaven itself. His enablement comes from the Word of God in the Bible, that "skillful and godly wisdom" that serves as its solid foundation. His hand is what makes our "secure dwellings" both peaceful and prosperous. Our surrender and obedience to the Lord in following His commands and behaving with integrity in all our actions is what opens the door to the blessings of the Lord.

Creating a home is so much more than physical furnishings or raising a family. The Lord wants to provide us a safety net, a place of wholeness and healing, a home where we know rest can truly be found. Paul wrote, "For we who believe [that is, we who personally trust and confidently rely on God] enter that rest [so we have His inner peace now because we are confident in our salvation, and assured of His power]" (Hebrews 4:3). Rest is also not just a physical state; it's a silent confidence that God is in control of all things. He alone is the "Builder of all things," whereby we are assured that our present and future are in His capable hands, and we can release worry and fear knowing that our foundation is sure. Our ultimate heavenly home gives us the hope that no matter what happens to us in our earthly lives, when we serve Jesus as our Lord, we can trust that He will carry our burdens *and* remove them completely in the end. Christ said,

> Come to Me, all who are weary and heavily burdened [by religious rituals that provide no peace], and I will give you rest [refreshing your souls with salvation]. Take My yoke

> upon you and learn from Me [following Me as My disciple], for I am gentle and humble in heart, and you will find rest (renewal, blessed quiet) for your souls. For My yoke is easy [to bear] and My burden is light. (Matthew 11:28-30)

I know how hard it is to feel like you carry the weight of the world on your shoulders. Life has a way of weighing us down daily, doesn't it? The enemy of our souls, Satan, wants us to feel that way because it keeps us from being productive and often from surrendering and obeying the Lord. The world tells us to be strong and independent, but we know the deep truth is that we are weak without the strength of God. So Jesus makes it easier for us by opening His arms and saying, "I am the rest you need." In *The Passion Translation* of the verse above, it says, "For I am your Oasis." Oh, that sounds good, right? I want an oasis to be my home on both the earth and in heaven!

The most wonderful part of giving our burdens over to the Lord is that now our hands are free to receive all that He has to offer us. While we rest from our struggles, we suddenly become aware that His blessing and favor lead us into seasons of joy. We are able to see and realize that He has given dreams and gifts for us all to walk out in our lives. God desires us to be faithful when the Holy Spirit shows us the steps to take in that direction. We're called to be faithful to Him in every thought, word, and action, to the best of our ability, all from the safety net of His rest. Romans 12:1-2 (MSG) says:

> So here's what I want you to do, God helping you: Take your everyday, ordinary life—your sleeping, eating, going-to-work, and walking-around life—and place it before God as an offering. Embracing what God does for you is the best thing you can do for him. Don't become so well-adjusted to your culture that you fit into it without even thinking. Instead, fix your attention on God. You'll be changed from the inside out. ***Readily recognize what he wants from you, and quickly respond to it.*** Unlike the culture around you, always dragging you down to its level of immaturity, God brings the best out of you, develops well-formed maturity in you. (emphasis added)

As we learn to navigate this life of faith, all God asks of us is to see it through to the end until He ushers us into His home. Learning how to recognize how God speaks to us and obeying Him when He does are the challenge. This sounds easy, but it's truly one of the hardest things I've ever done. It can be difficult to let go and trust when He only reveals our next step when we'd prefer to see the whole path. I'm sorry to say, God rarely provides us with all that information, which is why faith is absolutely essential. As it says in Hebrews 11:1, faith is having confidence in what we hope for and assurance about what we do not see. I've found that showing us just one step at a time helps to build our faith and trust. More of the path may be intimidating, or maybe you'd rush forward and leave Him behind. Either way, it's essential to know God intimately, get as close to

Him as humanly possible, and then surrender to His overall plan. It is that space in which we are home.

One of my favorite women of faith, Elisabeth Elliot, quoted an old poem when she said, "Do the next [right] thing."[14] I recently read that "Sometimes faithfulness is doing the hard thing because you know it's the right thing. Other times faithfulness might feel like blind trust, stumbling in the dark searching for light."[15] That is the simple act of obedience, even if you only see the one step in front of you. Just taking that one step is your act of surrendered obedience while trusting God to be the light to your path.

God is most concerned about our hearts and how we relate to Him and others in our lives. Prayer is where our relationship with the Lord begins, the place He starts building the foundation of our earthly spiritual home. He will take us on from there, overflowing His love in our hearts in order to bring that love to others. We also learn what He asks of us by reading the Bible, every word of which is God-breathed and written as a love letter to us. Jesus says, "But if you make yourselves at home with me and my words are at home in you, you can be sure that whatever you ask will be listened to and acted upon. This is how my Father shows who he is" (John 15:7-8, MSG). On this heaven-bound journey, God shows us who He is over and over by what He does and how He speaks to us. He listens intently to every prayer we pray. He takes note of our "coming and going"

---

14 Sutphen, Eleanor Amerman. "Ye Nexte Thynge." Fleming H. Revell Company, 1897.

15 Scarlet, Sarah. [@_sarahscarlet]. *Instagram*, 4 Apr. 2023, https://www.instagram.com/_sarahscarlet/p/CqoYxYEr0BV/?utm_.

LORD

(Psalm 121:8, NIV), considering the alignment of our hearts with His Word. He also gives us the beautiful benefit of grace when we fall short of this desire. When our spiritual lives are in alignment with His will, He'll mercifully instruct our next steps, help us leave behind the past, and walk onward in His light with us until we are finally *home*.

## Choice Challenge

Have you ever felt your inner voice cry out, "I want to go home"? Have you searched for that *home*? Have you considered that the only *home* you really need is God? Can you release your heart into His capable hands, walk His way, and find your true Home? Journal about your thoughts of home—what that has been for you, what it would mean to you to find that in God, and how you can respond to His "homing signal" in your daily choices and, even more so, in the life-changing ones.

## Prayer

*Dear Father, I long to know that You are really there and that You really do care. Please help me believe that You have good plans for my life here on earth, as well as in heaven. Help me to run with perseverance the race You have called me to in this life, one surrendered, obedient step at a time. Please help me be faithful and loyal to Your heart alone so I can find my way home. In Jesus' name, Amen.*

## Choice #6 – Out With the Old, In With the New?

It's been said that "The clothes make the man" (or woman). Now, I don't condone judgment based on clothing, but I do recognize that clothes can communicate a cultural and social significance to the world around us. Frankly, I don't think I ever understood this until I found my wedding gown. I felt like a princess bride from the moment I zipped it up. I actually couldn't believe I pulled it off the rack, and it fit me perfectly without needing any alterations. For me, when I saw myself in the mirror, however, it was not as much about the dress as it was about what it represented. I was going to be Mrs. Alex Compton, and just as that dress fit me perfectly, I knew I was the only one meant to be Alex's wife. The excitement that held was indescribable. A grin illuminated my face as I basked in the sea of possibilities of what our life together could be. I felt completely relaxed and elated all at the same time. I had found my person, my other half, the one whom my soul loves!

The prophet Isaiah wrote, "I will rejoice greatly in the Lord, my soul will exult in my God; for He has clothed me with garments of salvation, He has covered me with a robe of righteousness, as a bridegroom puts on a turban, and as a bride adorns herself with her jewels" (Isaiah 61:10). It's a glorious image, isn't it? A bride dressed for her wedding with precious gems and fine clothing, ready to begin a new life with her bridegroom. This is exactly how I felt the day I bought my dress—which just happened to be Valentine's Day. I was overwhelmed with joy because my life was being given a new purpose. I would no longer be living for myself, be responsible for only myself, or make choices however I saw fit for myself. This beautiful dress I wore marked the promise of a new day, a new adventure, a whole new journey more amazing than I could ever imagine alone.

In much the same way, our "spiritual clothes" also "make the (wo)man." When we choose to place our faith in Christ, we take on the "clothing of salvation," meaning we believe Jesus has saved us from the power of sin and death. In place of old clothing, we take on Christ's "robe of righteousness." His robe is free of sin, and once we put it on, God the Father sees us as pure, unblemished by sin. In this, we choose to leave behind our self-defeating actions, our poor choices, all things that lead to curses and death, so that we can walk into victorious, abundant life. We're given a new purpose in life. The apostle Paul wrote to the Galatians, "But now you have arrived at your destination: By faith in Christ, you are in direct relationship with God. Your baptism in Christ was not just washing you up for a fresh start. It also involved dressing you in an adult faith wardrobe—Christ's life, the fulfillment of God's original promise" (Galatians 3:25-27, MSG). Putting on our "adult faith wardrobe" is the place of transition from living and believing in old ways to living as a believer in the person of Jesus Christ, as we choose daily to follow Him as Lord and be clothed by His character.

Paul described these new "clothes" to the Colossians:

> Your old life is dead. Your new life, which is your *real* life—even though invisible to spectators—is with Christ in God. *He* is your life. When Christ (your real life, remember)

shows up again on this earth, you'll show up, too—the real you, the glorious you. Meanwhile, be content with obscurity, like Christ. And that means killing off everything connected with that way of death: sexual promiscuity, impurity, lust, doing whatever you feel like whenever you feel like it, and grabbing whatever attracts your fancy. That's a life shaped by things and feelings instead of by God. It's because of this kind of thing that God is about to explode in anger. It wasn't long ago that you were doing all that stuff and not knowing any better. But you know better now, so make sure it's all gone for good: bad temper, irritability, meanness, profanity, dirty talk. Don't lie to one another. You're done with that old life. It's like a filthy set of ill-fitting clothes you've stripped off and put in the fire. Now you're dressed in a new wardrobe. Every item of your new way of life is custom-made by the Creator, with his label on it. All the old fashions are now obsolete. Words like Jewish and non-Jewish, religious and irreligious, insider and outsider, uncivilized and uncouth, slave and free, mean nothing. From now on everyone is defined by Christ, everyone is included in Christ. So, chosen by God for this new life of love, dress in the wardrobe God picked out for you: compassion, kindness, humility, quiet strength, discipline. Be even-tempered,

> content with second place, quick to forgive an offense. Forgive as quickly and completely as the Master forgave you. And regardless of what else you put on, wear love. It's your basic, all-purpose garment. Never be without it. (Colossians 3:3-14, MSG)

Choosing to put our faith in Jesus as our Savior is the single most important step of our lives. The next step is submitting to Jesus as Lord of our life. And that means we get to put on these new clothes of compassion, kindness, humility, strength, etc. We choose daily to get rid of anger, rage, slander, filthy language, etc. This is what will define the life we now live, a life that is not self-focused, not self-contained, but a life that is lived for others, along with a consistent and bold focus on embracing those who still may wear old clothes. Love is the most essential garment to wear because that is how Jesus was clothed every day of His earthly life. His clothing, His character, was defined by His love for you.

It may be acceptable in the world's standards to judge a person by what they look like, but that was never how Christ evaluated others. To Him, only the heart matters:

> Your adornment must not be merely external—with interweaving and elaborate knotting of the hair, and wearing gold jewelry, or [being superficially preoccupied with] dressing in expensive clothes; but let it be [the inner beauty of] the hidden person of the heart, with the imperishable quality and unfading charm of a gentle and peaceful

> spirit, [one that is calm and self-controlled, not overanxious, but serene and spiritually mature] which is very precious in the sight of God. For in this way in former times the holy women, who hoped in God, used to adorn themselves, being submissive to their own husbands and adapting themselves to them. (1 Peter 3:3-5)

Have you ever met someone who immediately gave you the impression that they had a "gentle and peaceful spirit" or were "serene and spiritually mature"? Have you ever gotten to know them better and found that their "inner beauty of the hidden person of the heart" came from the God you now serve? If not, I bet you would find that these kinds of people have surrendered their lives to the Lord. You'd find that they don't focus on fancy jewelry or expensive clothes. You'd find that the "imperishable quality and unfading charm" they exude comes from knowing the Lord, the Creator of the universe, in an intimate way. They have found their peace and rest in Him and trust Him as Lord to care for their lives, while releasing worry and fear. You'd find that they are "calm and self-controlled, not overanxious," because the attitude of their hearts is like the attitude of worship that Jesus had towards His own Father. They want to live like Jesus lived and love like Jesus loved. Those are the people who stand out in this world and act as a doorway to the eternal.

At the end of Jesus' earthly life, He told His disciples, "I am giving you a new commandment, that you love one another. Just as I have loved you, so you too are to love one another. By this everyone will know that you are My disciples, if you have love and unselfish concern for one another" (John 13:34-35). The amazing result of being well dressed with Christ's character on the inside is that it's eventually reflected on the outside. When we are confident in our relationship with Jesus as Lord, that confidence cannot be hidden on the surface. Just as I began glowing as a bride-to-be, having been loved and chosen to be the wife of an amazing man of God, we cannot hide the truth of the transformation in our hearts from *water* to *wine*. It is truly a transformation worth celebrating.

## Choice Challenge

Are you prepared to release the old "clothes" in your life and be redefined by Christ's garment of salvation and robe of righteousness? This is an essential step of leaving the *water* life behind and embracing the *wine* life. Will you allow the old ways to die off, to put on Love, and walk in the new way of a gentle and quiet spirit? Write down three types of "old clothes" that you want Christ to exchange for new ones. (For instance, extending forgiveness to someone, replacing some of your questionable vocabulary choices, or not offering a hand gesture to an offensive driver.)

## Prayer

*Dear Father, I'm ready for a new wardrobe. Take all my old labels, all the clothes I no longer need, and replace them with Your finest! Help me to surrender my spirit to You and trust You to make the changes that need to be made. I want to live out this new adventure with the character and love of Christ. In Jesus' name, Amen.*

## *Chapter 3.*

# OBEY

"Charlie" was my alter ego as a teenager. My grandfather used to call me that, so I took it as a nickname at age 14 because there were two other girls named Holly in my circle of friends. But it became more than just a nickname; Charlie was the sneaky rebel, defiantly choosing her own terms under the radar. Holly, on the other hand, was the A+ girl, leading from the front, masquerading compliance, and gaining onlooker approval. You get it, right? The real me just didn't want to be the good little girl and do what I was told.

But when Charlie met Jesus, she had to "come and die." I had to choose His way or mine. Humility had to overcome arrogance. Charlie was never truly satisfied, as much as she sought it in food or other methods of filling the void within. When she met the Holy Spirit head-on, she realized that it was His way or the highway:

> I say, then, walk by the Spirit and you will certainly not carry out the desire of the flesh. For the flesh desires what is against the Spirit, and the Spirit desires what is against the flesh; these are opposed to each other, so

> that you don't do what you want. (Galatians 5:16-17, CSB)

We are all flesh-controlled creatures motivated by pleasure and humanly cravings. By nature, we are compelled to do that which satisfies ourselves, and we are resistant to the control of others who may hinder the immediate satisfaction of our fleshly needs. So when the Spirit of God insists we not pursue instant gratification, surrender is rarely our first response.

As God gave me glimpses of Himself in Scripture, I knew that He was what I really needed. Then I would close my eyes and envision Jesus looking at me with such unconditional acceptance, I readily gave up Charlie in a heartbeat. I chose to respond to His will and guidance so that I could find that *wine* life, and I believe you can, too.

Remember, if it were easy, everyone would do it. The "come and die" life isn't for the weak-willed, my friend. It takes daily choices to surrender and obey, to do things His way so that He gets the glory and we find that which truly satisfies. And oh my goodness, it is so worth it.

## Choice #7 - Blessed or Stressed?

"Expect blessing," she said, as I conquered the elliptical trainer at the gym with the TV tuned into Joyce Meyer's "Enjoying Everyday Life" program. Joyce said that every day is a gift from God, which He is eager to give us if we simply ask Him for it. There's no special formula or prayer; just ask for His blessing, and trust Him to come through.[16]

16 *Enjoying Everyday Life*, hosted by Joyce Meyer, Trinity Broadcasting Network.

Well, that day happened to be my $26^{th}$ birthday, and I sincerely needed a new job. So I asked God to bless me with a phone call about a new job opportunity that day—and He did, indeed, bless me with exactly that. The following week when I prepared to interview, I remembered that my husband was offered a job on the same day he interviewed just a month earlier. So I asked God to bless me with a job offer that same day—and He did, indeed, bless me with exactly that!

Best job I ever had, too.

Are God's blessings flowing in your life? If you're reading this book, then I know that He has blessed you enough to put this book in your hands and speak to your heart about drawing closer to Him in some way. If you can read at all, you are more blessed than 773 million people worldwide who are illiterate, two-thirds of whom are women.[17] If you ate a meal today, you are more blessed than 673 million people worldwide who did not.[18] But even all of these people are blessed to have breath in their lungs and the opportunity to know God in this life.

God longs and loves to be intimately involved with our journey from surviving as *water* to thriving as *wine*. His hand touches us, and we are ever transforming. God's blessings flow more easily when we choose to have the

---

17 "773 Million People Worldwide Would Not Be Able to Read This Article." *Action Education*, 8 Sept. 2023, https://action-education.org/en/773-million-people-not-read-this-article/. Accessed 7 Feb. 2026.

18 *"World Hunger Facts." Action Against Hunger*, Action Against Hunger USA, https://www.actionagainsthunger.org/the-hunger-crisis/world-hunger-facts/. Accessed 7 Feb. 2026.

Lord in our lives. Even when we walk through the valleys of life, God can adjust our perspective to see His hand touching our lives and to help us realize His blessings are still present. But seeking His blessings alone is not the goal. Brian Simmons writes:

> When we choose to walk with God, the way of peace is easy to find. When we become more satisfied with our relationship with God than the promise of his blessing, we set ourselves up for something far greater. No sacrifice will ever outweigh the glory of remaining close to him. Holding our promises loosely, knowing that God is ultimately in control, frees us to rest and enjoy him. Otherwise, we get fixated on temporal desires and are willing to fight and strive to get them. Let's posture our hearts before the Lord in humble faith. Humility is the precursor for his richest blessings.[19]

Our temporal blessings are not the endgame; knowing God the Father is the biggest blessing we could possibly have in this life. Why? Because that's all we can take into the next one. If heaven is our goal, knowing God is the reason for it and the only way to get there. The best way to know God in this world starts with reading His Word:

> What delight comes to the one who follows God's ways! ...His passion is to remain true to **the Word** of "I AM," **meditating day and night on the true revelation of light**. He

---

19 Simmons, Brian, and Gretchen Rodriguez. "Humility Leads to Blessing." *Firstfruits*. BroadStreet Publishing Group LLC, 2020.

> will be standing firm like a flourishing tree planted by God's design, deeply rooted by the brooks of bliss, bearing fruit in every season of life. He is never dry, never fainting, ever blessed, ever prosperous. (Psalm 1:1-4, TPT, emphasis added)

God is telling us that His Word is the "true revelation of light," the source of all He is, has always been, and will always be. He is unchanging, and He alone is the prize for which we run the race. Only knowing Him intimately leads to being "ever blessed, ever prosperous." But it all begins with our choice to surrender to His hands: "Your favor will fall like rain upon our surrendered lives, like showers reviving the earth. In the days of his reign the righteous will spring forth with the abundance of peace and prosperity forevermore" (Psalm 72:6-7, TPT). Surrendering to His ways, we receive reviving and abundant peace, while all of our steps "are directed and established by the Lord, and He delights in [our] way [and blesses our path]" (Psalm 37:23, pronouns modified). He has "stored up so many good things for us, like a treasure chest heaped up and spilling over with blessings—all for those who honor and worship [Him]!" (Psalm 31:19, TPT, pronoun modified).

Following our surrender to the Father, His call is for our obedience. Many times, this step is the most frustrating because we either think we don't know what He's asking us to do, or we do know but think it's too hard. Priscilla Shirer describes obedience this way:

> Facing up to this issue of obedience is the alpha and omega of how we hear from God.

> Obedience isn't just one of the keys. It is *the* key that unlocks all of the blessings God intends for us. It also keeps the door of communication with Him clear and continually open.[20]

If we are unsure as to what the Lord asks of us in a particular situation that has no definitive instruction in His Word, thankfully we can communicate with Him clearly and continually, waiting patiently for His distinctive answers. Here is where we can exercise our ability to discern His will for us and discern the next right thing to do to get there. While we wait, we are to faithfully do two things: choose to walk in His ways and choose to bless others. "Those who live to bless others will have blessings heaped upon them, and the one who pours out his life to pour out blessings will be saturated with favor" (Proverbs 11:25, TPT).

To be clear, to receive God's blessings, to make that transition from *water* to *wine*, we surrender and obey, while we are "recognizing [more clearly] the grace of our Lord Jesus Christ [His astonishing kindness, His generosity, His gracious favor], that though He was rich, yet for [our] sake He became poor, so that by His poverty [we] might become rich (abundantly blessed) (2 Corinthians 8:9, pronouns modified).

However, this is ***not*** a recipe for monetary riches on this earth. While His blessings *may* ***include*** financial prosperity, especially if that area of our lives is fully surrendered to His control, it doesn't guarantee we'll all be millionaires. God's "generosity" and "gracious favor" will take on countless

20 Shirer, *Discerning the Voice of God.*

forms, some of which are obvious to the naked eye—food, clothing, homes, jobs, raises, bonuses, unexpected checks in the mail—but the majority of what He offers us because of His "astonishing kindness" will only be found in our hearts and evidenced by our actions and where our hearts lead us.

The most important choice anyone ever made that would affect all of humanity was Jesus' choice to die for us. Jesus made Himself nothing, gave up His very life, so that we could have everything—eternal life with the Father *and* abundant blessings *now*. But what are those blessings? Here is an expanded glimpse of Matthew 5 from the Amplified Bible, which includes various words and phrases in brackets that help further clarify the meaning of the original texts, taking into consideration the original Greek, cultural implications, context, and nuances. This passage is known as the Beatitudes, where Jesus talks about what it means to be blessed:

> **Blessed [spiritually prosperous, happy, to be admired]** are the poor in spirit [those devoid of spiritual arrogance, those who regard themselves as insignificant], for theirs is the kingdom of heaven [both now and forever].
>
> **Blessed [forgiven, refreshed by God's grace]** are those who mourn [over their sins and repent], for they will be comforted [when the burden of sin is lifted].
>
> **Blessed [inwardly peaceful, spiritually secure, worthy of respect]** are the gentle

[the kind-hearted, the sweet-spirited, the self-controlled], for they will inherit the earth.

**Blessed [joyful, nourished by God's goodness]** are those who hunger and thirst for righteousness [those who actively seek right standing with God], for they will be [completely] satisfied.

**Blessed [content, sheltered by God's promises]** are the merciful, for they will receive mercy.

**Blessed [anticipating God's presence, spiritually mature]** are the pure in heart [those with integrity, moral courage, and godly character], for they will see God.

**Blessed [spiritually calm with life-joy in God's favor]** are the makers and maintainers of peace, for they will [express His character and] be called the sons of God.

**Blessed [comforted by inner peace and God's love]** are those who are persecuted for doing that which is morally right, for theirs is the kingdom of heaven [both now and forever].

**Blessed [morally courageous and spiritually alive with life-joy in God's goodness]** are you when people insult you and persecute you, and falsely say all kinds of evil things against you because of [your

> association with] Me. Be glad and exceedingly joyful, for your reward in heaven is great [absolutely inexhaustible]; for in this same way they persecuted the prophets who were before you. (Matthew 5:3-12, emphasis added)

That is a mouthful by itself, even without the statements that follow each "Blessed" definition. As we read through it all, we can comprehend through our faith that we are forgiven and spiritually secure. Beyond that, we are "spiritually mature" and "prosperous," which points toward being calm, peaceful, alive, happy, joyful, and content. Every one of those words builds on the next to prove how we are "sheltered by God's promises" and "nourished by God's goodness."

Being this blessed is not automatic; it is not a given in life. It is the result of choices that honor God, beginning with the choice to have a personal, saving relationship with Jesus Christ as Lord over our lives. That relationship signals the rebirth of our hearts, the choice that breathes life back into our dead spirits. We begin to anticipate God's presence and favor in our lives, but most beautifully, we become "morally courageous and spiritually alive with life-joy in God's goodness."

Life-joy. This is how we find real happiness. Not a fleeting day-to-day happiness, but a true joy that sustains us at our core. As one who has struggled with a lifetime of depression, I can grasp the unbelief that can erupt at the thought of finding this life-joy. God comes alongside us, comforts us with inner peace and His love, and births that life-joy within us that we choose to hold onto despite our circumstances. And as that life-joy begins to overflow in our lives into the lives of those around us, then we are even further blessed—"to be admired" and "worthy of respect." In the book *Blessed Are the Chosen*, Amanda Jenkins and her coauthors write:

> In the Sermon on the Mount, Jesus describes our new reality—our actual reality, regardless of our circumstances. He describes things we can't always see but remain true anyway; a kingdom not visible to the unsaved or spiritually untrained eye, but when brought into focus, provides hope that supersedes the hard things. In His sermon, Jesus describes the truth about what matters: who we are when we belong to Him, what we have when we belong to Him, where we're going because we belong to Him, and what it means to be blessed in the in-between and unto eternity. **Which means congratulations are in order. God's favor is upon you.**[21]

We may be in the "in-between"—knowing Jesus now while awaiting eternity with Him, but we don't have to wait for heaven to receive His blessings. Jesus said, "If you know these things, you are blessed [happy and favored by God] if you put them into practice [and faithfully do them]" (John 13:17). We release and submit our hearts to God, choosing to carefully follow His instructions, and He provides all these blessings afresh every day. While our circumstances may change, we never lack for anything. He is a good, good Father.

21 Jenkins, Amanda, et al. *Blessed Are the Chosen*. David C. Cook, 2022.

## Choice Challenge

Do you want God's blessings to flow abundantly in your life? Do you recognize the ways they already do? Will you surrender and obey Him with your whole heart? Will you choose to walk in His ways and to bless others? Will you start each day with gratitude and feed the part of you that lives only for Him? Thank Him for His blessings now by making a list of as many blessings you can think of, tangible or otherwise.

**Prayer**

*Dear Father, I am so grateful for all the blessings You have already poured out in my life. I choose to surrender and obey; open my ears to hear Your voice and my heart to receive Your instructions. Draw me closer to Your heart each day. Thank You for Your kindness and Your promises to bless me as I walk closely with You and according to Your ways. In Jesus' name, Amen.*

## Choice #8 – Listen AND Obey?

A year before getting married, Alex and I began working with a missions organization in Peru. On our first short-term mission trip, we spent about 10 days with a team of over 200 people in San Juan de Lurigancho, a town outside Lima. There, our team split up to visit many parts of the city for various kinds of service. Some groups held free medical, dental, and vision clinics, some performed dramas in the streets that shared the message of salvation, while Alex and I participated in conferences to encourage and share Christ with men, women, and pastors. During that trip, Alex and I easily fell in love with the welcoming and generous Peruvian people. We talked about one day returning for another mission trip after we were married.

A year after our wedding, we were settling into bed on Easter Sunday evening. Alex looked at me and asked, "If God told you to sell all of your things and move to another country, would you do it?"

Without hesitation, I emphatically exclaimed, "No way!" My almost autonomic reflex instantly cycled through his proposition's requirements: selling our belongings, relinquishing our American comforts, and sacrificing careers and friendships in order to undertake such a crazy and fearful task. Well, as bizarre and untimely as Alex's question arose, it was stranger still that he said nothing further, rolled over, and promptly fell asleep. Truly caught off guard by his puzzling question, I could barely fall asleep myself. I said *no*, I meant *no*, and I wanted to forget his suggestion entirely.

However, God had in mind a different proposal. He woke me up for several hours in the middle of the next three nights so He could communicate an opposing plan. On the third sleepless night, God put this thought in my head: *Holly, if you stay, you will always stay. If you go, you will always go.* In my heart, I knew, obedience was the only road for me.

On Wednesday morning, as we prepared for our day, I gathered his attention and said, “We’re moving to Peru, babe.”

“Do what, now?” Alex said, although his demeanor wasn’t one of surprise.

“I’m going to teach English in Peru, and you’re going to oversee the short-term mission teams and general projects.”

Alex simply looked at me with a smile and said, “God told me the same thing on Easter morning. I told Him that if it were really Him speaking, He would have to tell you word-for-word what He told me. And it looks like He did just that.”

Well, it would seem that God was not done communicating the agenda with me. In fact, my midnight rendezvous with the Father continued nightly for three months straight. While I begrudgingly sacrificed my sleep, each encounter helped conform and prepare my soul for the tasks ahead. God sought ongoing cooperation that gave Him permission to change my ways of thinking, just in time for me to obediently walk forward into our Peruvian destiny that would unfold over the next decade.

Hearing the voice of God is not as easy as it sounds, especially if we haven't had much practice listening for it. God is such a loving, merciful Father. He is always speaking to each and every one of us, and we simply must learn to recognize it over time. Most people don't hear an audible voice when God speaks. It's often just a passing thought in our minds, but it carries the weight of a holy Author. Meaning, we recognize that the thought was not our own, and action is required on our part to obey. If this is something you're struggling with, remember, there's grace for learning how to "decode" the Holy Spirit within you. Anne Graham Lotz, daughter of Billy Graham, wrote in her book, *The Daniel Key*, "Why do you think it's hard to hear from God? Maybe the problem isn't with His voice. Maybe the problem is with your ears. It's time to make the choice to listen daily as you open your Bible and read it."[22] Recognizing the beauty of His "voice" takes practice, but every minute we spend learning His tone and character in the Bible helps us to fluently discern His message to us more easily.

Because we are aware of God's eyes on us, we can trust that He is able to show us what His will is. He knows if we need to turn left or right, stand up or sit down, speak up or keep quiet. Psalm 32:8 says, "I will instruct you and teach you in the way you should go; I will counsel you [who are willing to learn] with My eye upon you." This is a special promise He has made us, that He won't abandon us to fend for ourselves, to figure anything out all alone—He's available, and He's *not* hiding His perfect will from us.

---

22 Lotz, Anne Graham. *The Daniel Key: 20 Choices That Make All the Difference*. Zondervan, 2018.

The prophet Isaiah even wrote, "Your ears will hear a word behind you, 'This is the way, walk in it,' whenever you turn to the right or to the left" (Isaiah 30:21). He has already seen the outcome of our choices and knows the best ones for us to take. He comes alongside us and leads us, intimately and ever so personally.

But—can we discern that voice amidst a very loud, distracting world? When life feels chaotic and demanding, we might even allow ourselves to drown out the voice of the Lord. Thankfully, we serve a God who knows how frail we are, so we can trust Him to speak with a gentle, alluring, and unhurried voice. In the midst of any storm, we can choose to tune in to Him for guidance and refuge.

In 2020, I read a beautiful allegory called *Hinds Feet on High Places* by Hannah Hurnard, which describes a beautiful scene where the Shepherd (Jesus) is speaking to the sojourner, known as "Much-Afraid":

> My sheep hear my voice and they follow me. Whenever you are willing to obey me, Much-Afraid, and to follow the path of my choice, you will always be able to hear and recognize my voice, and when you hear it you must always obey. Remember also that it is always safe to obey my voice, even if it seems to call you to paths which look impossible or even crazy.[23]

God the Father is kind and handles our souls with tender care. He wants us to trust Him and what He says,

23 Hurnard, Hannah. *Hinds' Feet on High Places: An Engaging Visual Journey*. Tyndale House Publishers, 1975.

even if it seems scary. One instruction that has often troubled me, especially as an introvert, is when I sense God leading me to speak up about truly *anything*. I might be in a private conversation with someone, in a small group or classroom setting of some kind, or even in front of a church congregation. I don't have a fear of public speaking, but I do have a fear of being wrong or rejected. Listening and obeying are all God asks of me. The results belong to the Holy Spirit, who always works all things together, to bless someone who hears whatever I'm supposed to say.

Jim Cymbala said:

> Our spiritual ear will never be sensitive to his voice if we have a personal agenda to which we are already committed. God leads and speaks to the humble who have surrendered their plans and want to do His will. With an "open heaven" and a surrendered will, we will be able to clearly hear God's voice in our hearts.[24]

Do something with me. Hold out your hand with a flat palm facing upward. If we present open hands to Him, imagine how He can easily give us whatever is necessary in our lives. Open hands also allow Him to sovereignly *take away* harmful things or people we'd rather hold onto more tightly, causing us to grieve at times. Grieving loss is never easy, but God says He is our constant companion throughout the grieving process. If we continue to offer up those open hands even when it hurts, He is also able to give us instructions, provided that we put aside our own

24 Shirer, *Discerning the Voice of God.*

intentions, agendas, and desires, not just once in a while, but all the time.

Hearing from the Lord is contingent upon our surrendered, open hands. Priscilla Shirer wrote, “Immediate obedience creates the needed margin for God to invade our everyday lives, to stir up supernatural activity, to cause our hearts to pound with anticipation, and to ruin us for ‘church’ as usual.”[25] Radical obedience, as she suggests, means we don’t spend our days and nights doing our own thing, but rather, we give God permission to jump into our timetables at any point, mix things up, and make our faith authentically active on any day of the week, not just on Sundays.

A heart that loves the Lord and stands surrendered to His instructions is an important prerequisite to hearing His voice. Patience and persistence also open our spiritual ears. He may not answer our prayers immediately, but He has promised that we will find the answers in some way. Matthew 5:4 (TPT) says, “What delight comes to you when you wait upon the Lord! For you will find what you long for.” Throughout our lives, we discover that waiting on Him is the most demanding but most meaningful, even monumental task God asks of us, but He promises us that He’s big enough, sees enough, knows more than enough, to answer at the perfect time and in the perfect manner. In seasons of waiting, when my faith feels thin, I cling to a poem by J.J. Lynch, called “Say Not, My Soul”:

---

25 Shirer, *Discerning the Voice of God.*

Say not, my soul, 'From whence
Can God relieve my care?'
Remember that Omnipotence
Hath servants everywhere.

His help is always sure,
His methods seldom guessed;
Delay will make our pleasure pure;
Surprise will give it zest.

*His wisdom is sublime,*
*His heart profoundly kind;*
*God never is before His time,*
*and never is behind.*

Hast thou assumed a load
Which none will bear with thee?
And art thou bearing it for God,
And shall He fail to see?[26]

That third stanza speaks volumes to the importance of trusting God's wisdom and kindness in the midst of anxious impatience. As He grows our patience, He prepares us to receive His answers. He may speak through a Scripture, a circumstance, another person, a poem, a song, or countless other possibilities, as long as we have our hands and ears open to receive what He offers.

In Revelation 3:20 (TPT), Jesus says: "Behold, I'm standing at the door, knocking. If your heart is open to hear

26 Lynch, Thomas T. "Say Not, My Soul." *The Disciplines of Life*. World Wide Publications, 1948. (emphasis added)

my voice and you open the door within, I will come in to you and feast with you, and you will feast with me." Jesus has a sweet and humble voice, and His loving demeanor is not a mystical or mythical thing—He is truly before us with open arms to receive us into His embrace. We may still struggle to do as He asks, when He asks, but the possibility alone of obedience is how we invite Jesus in to lead us. This is where we humble ourselves in surrender and trust that His will is best. This is when we choose Life.

## Choice Challenge

Let's be real here. Are you convinced that God's will is better than your own? Start there; don't gloss over that question. Are you *convinced* that God's will is far better than what you can even imagine? Because it is. Knowing that, will you choose to obey when instruction is given? Before God answers your prayer, will you commit to doing what He is requiring of you? Write down a few areas in your life where you need direction from God, like how to spend money or whether or not to relocate; then ask Him to make the Holy Spirit's direction clear to you.

## Prayer

*Dear Father, trusting You is a daily journey that I am taking step by step. I come to You with open hands. Take what You need to take; give what You need to give. Help me to hear Your voice with an expectant, willing heart; help me choose Your path, not my own. You are the right Way! I choose the right Way, Lord. In Jesus' name, Amen.*

## Choice #9 – Your Body or His Temple?

Someone once told me that if you struggle with discipline, try doing one new thing every day for a month, and you'll lay the foundation for a new habit. I picked making my bed. I realized that after that first month, the new habit wasn't what made me continue to make my bed. What mattered was how making my bed every day made me feel. As a goal-oriented person, I am very orderly in my approach to getting from point A to point B. (It blesses me greatly that God is also orderly and not a God of chaos.) When I do things in an organized way, I feel more at peace with my circumstances and in relation to others involved. So when I make my bed, the beginning of my day is off to an orderly start, followed by my regular daily routine. Having my bed made also invites me into a peaceful evening when it's time to sleep again.

Discipline in caring for our physical bodies is very much the same. It's not the specific habits, per say, although making good choices in regard to eating and exercise is essential, but it's the result of the habits that makes us continue to walk them out daily. When we choose to feed our bodies healthful food and get regular exercise at our personal level of ability, the result is a healthy body that generally has a solid level of energy and a fortified immune system. Having a healthy body then makes us available to God for Him to use us in any way He sees fit without any impediment to His purpose or design. This is God's call in our lives when we turn our hearts over to Him, according to 1 Corinthians:

> Have you forgotten that your body is now the sacred temple of the Spirit of Holiness, who lives in you? You don't belong to yourself any longer, for the gift of God, the Holy Spirit, lives inside your sanctuary. You were God's expensive purchase, paid for with tears of blood, so by all means, then, use your body to bring glory to God! (1 Corinthians 6:19-20, TPT)

When we welcome Jesus into our lives as Savior and as Lord, the Holy Spirit comes to live in our hearts. With God living within us, we are His "temple," the sacred space where He dwells, which is holy and set apart for His purposes. We surrender our mind, will, and emotions to the Father; doing so with our bodies is also necessary. This kind of surrender generates a moment-by-moment crossroads where we can use our bodies to walk in God's ways, or not. Healthy disciplines follow with God's instructions in this area, in Matthew 6:31-34 (TPT), when Jesus says:

> So then, forsake your worries! Why would you say, "What will we eat?" or "What will we drink?" or "What will we wear?" For that is what the unbelievers chase after. Doesn't your heavenly Father already know the things your bodies require? So above all, constantly seek God's kingdom and his righteousness, then all these less important things will be given to you abundantly. Refuse to worry about tomorrow, but deal with each challenge that

> comes your way, one day at a time. Tomorrow will take care of itself.

Our Lord's assurance of His provision and abundance is available to all of us when we put Him first. He alone is our Master; we cannot allow the things "the unbelievers chase after," like food or clothes, to become our idols. Those things are simply a means to an end—God's glory—when our desires and dreams are fully submitted to His reign. We remember that His sovereignty is what brings all of it together into the fantastic tapestry that He weaves with our lives as a whole. His ultimate goal is blessing those whom He loves and who love Him, as Proverbs illustrates:

> Don't think for a moment that you know it all, for wisdom comes when you adore him with undivided devotion and avoid everything that's wrong. Then you will find the healing refreshment your body and spirit long for. (Proverbs 3:7-8, TPT)

Admitting we *don't* know it all is freeing, isn't it? I would rather trust an unknown future to a known God, and not the other way around. If our devotion to Him is undivided, we will find the refreshing satisfaction in mind and body that only God can provide.

## Choice Challenge

Is physical discipline a struggle for you? How well do you care for your body? If the Spirit of God lives within you, are you surrendering your body to Him for His exclusive use? Will you let Him teach you new habits so that your body can be used for His glory? Write down one new habit you could adopt for the next 21 days and why you chose it. Keep track of the days you complete it or don't and how it affects your days. Then bring it back to God and pray for His perspective on the results.

**Prayer**

*Dear Father, I confess I have not always used my body for Your holy purposes. Please forgive me for not treating my body as Your temple. I surrender my body, my physical habits, and my discipline choices to You, Lord. Please come in and make whatever renovations are necessary for You to use this temple for Your glory alone. In Jesus' name, Amen.*

# Part II

# Choosing True Life Happens From the Inside Out

This song, called "Forever Reign" by Hillsong Worship, draws us deeper into the heart of Jesus, where He can change everything deeper in us:

You are good / When there's nothing good in me...
You are love / On display for all to see...
You are light / When the darkness closes in...
You are hope / You have covered all my sins...

You are peace / When my fear is crippling...
You are truth / Even in my wondering...
You are joy / You're the reason that I sing...
You are ***life*** / In you death has lost its sting...

I'm running to your arms / The riches of your love will ***always*** be ***enough*** Nothing compares to your embrace / Light of the world / Forever reign

You are more / Than my words will ever say...
You are Lord / All creation will proclaim...
You are here / In your presence I'm made whole...
You are God / ***Of all else I'm letting go...***[27]

And then another song, called "From the Inside, Out," continues His work in our hearts:

...In my heart and my soul, Lord, ***I give You control***
Consume me from the inside out, Lord
Let justice and praise become my embrace
***To love You from the inside out...***[28]

27 Morgan, Reuben, and Jason Ingram. "Forever Reign," *A Beautiful Exchange*, Hillsong Music, 2010 (emphasis added).

28 Houston, Joel."From the Inside Out." *United We Stand (Live)*, Hillsong Music, 2006. (emphasis added)

Chapter 4

# WORDS

I can remember my first piece of writing that ever got noticed. I giggle when I think of the poem about a cat that my second-grade teacher thought was so amazing that she had it written on her chalkboard for everyone to see for a whole month. It made my classmates giggle, too, especially when they heard I didn't have a cat and made the whole thing up.

Words and the ability they have to build up or tear down people or situations have always captivated me. However, I don't think I really appreciated that until after I started following Jesus. If the Bible calls Him "*The* Word," I realized I needed to be much more careful with what came out of my mouth and what flowed out of my pen.

Do you struggle with this too? Maybe saying things you don't really mean in the heat of an argument? Or do you remember painful words that were spoken to you as a child that you rehearse time and again in your mind? I remember some I wish I didn't.

My point is, it's time to pour new, life-giving words that Jesus spoke into your heart through the Scriptures in the New Testament. You can find living words in the Old Testament descriptions of God's forgiving character, too. It's time to listen for those living words as He speaks transformation over you. Then you can use those living words to praise His name and to breathe those loving words over the people in your life who need a touch of Jesus too.

## Choice #10 – Will You Study?

In the summer of 1998, I felt truly crushed to the point of breathlessness for the first time in my life. I had hoped it would be the best summer of my life as I ventured far from home for a two-month mission trip to the opposite coast of Canada. It was the farthest I'd ever traveled away from home in my life, and I knew not a single soul on the trip with me. I packed up everything I could fit in one suitcase and backpack, including all my fears and hopes and excitement for the adventure to come.

Unfortunately, it didn't all go according to my perfect plan. Although I quickly made friends there in Vancouver, I was terribly homesick for Massachusetts. Then just two weeks in, I had a frightful fall, spraining my right knee and left ankle, forcing me to spend several weeks in a wheelchair. As the summer progressed, I made many long-distance calls home (with my mother's calling card—yikes!). I soon discovered that my parents had finalized their divorce, sold the house I grew up in, gave up *my* dog for adoption without any warning, and moved into separate apartments.

Yep. I told you it was bad.

For the entire following year, I desperately tried to be okay. Everything I once knew was now gone, but unwilling to face it all just yet, I shoved every emotion deep into my gut. The sadness swallowed me whole, and I chopped off almost all my hair as I dealt with the grief. I earnestly prayed that God would fulfill His promise in Psalm 34:18 (NLT), "The Lord is close to the brokenhearted, and He rescues those whose spirits are crushed." Like the good Father God is, He eventually sent a fellow missionary named John Paul to pray for me in the midst of my despair, and the spirit of darkness that taunted me day and night thankfully left (that's the short version of a year-long story). John Paul warned me to be careful of the darkness returning unless I fortified my own spirit with the Light, God's Word.

The Word tells us that our enemy, the devil, roams the earth looking for someone to devour. In John 10:10 (TPT), Jesus tells us, "A thief has only one thing in mind—he wants to steal, slaughter, and destroy. But I have come to give you everything in abundance, more than you expect—life in its fullness until you overflow!" Jesus warned us to be careful because the devil is a tangible and fervent threat to our souls, especially in the battlefield of our minds. However, He promised that there was much more to life than the devil's schemes. Jesus came to bless us more than we could ever expect in this world. We can trust Him at His Word. In John 16:33, Jesus also said:

> I have told you these things, so that in Me you may have [perfect] peace. In the world you have tribulation and distress and suffering, but be courageous [be confident, be undaunted, be filled with joy]; I have overcome the world. [My conquest is accomplished, My victory abiding.]

Jesus has the final say when it comes to victory over the enemy. He does warn us that while we live this life, we will, indeed, suffer. That is why the apostle Paul wrote to encourage us to wear Christ's spiritual armor in every battle with the enemy:

> In conclusion, be strong in the Lord [draw your strength from Him and be empowered through your union with Him] and in the power of His [boundless] might. Put on the full armor of God [for His precepts are like the splendid armor of a heavily-armed soldier], so that you may be able to [successfully] stand up against all the schemes and the strategies and the deceits of the devil. For our struggle is not against flesh and blood [contending only with physical opponents], but against the rulers, against the powers, against the world forces of this [present] darkness, against the spiritual forces of wickedness in the heavenly (supernatural) places. (Ephesians 6:10-12)

There may not be a physical battle for our souls (depending on what country you live in), but there most certainly is a spiritual one. The enemy wants more than anything to steal our hearts and remove our devotion to the Lord. If he can claim our souls, then he is able to claim our minds, our wills, and our emotions in one fell swoop. There is darkness looming around every corner: everything we take in through our senses can immediately bombard our hearts in unintentional ways, which we may not realize until it's too late. Whatever we see, hear, touch, and even taste can lead us astray. Our own sin chisels away at our love for the Lord, turning it over to the enemy a little bit at a time. This can lead to addictions of our fleshly desires that incrementally draw our devotion away from our Savior and toward crisis emotionally, mentally, and spiritually, if we do not stand guard. Paul goes on to say:

> Therefore, put on the complete armor of God, so that you will be able to [successfully] resist and stand your ground in the evil day [of danger], and having done everything [that the crisis demands], to stand firm [in your place, fully prepared, immovable, victorious]. So stand firm and hold your ground, having tightened the wide band of truth (personal integrity, moral courage) around your waist and having put on the breastplate of righteousness (an upright heart), and having strapped on your feet the gospel of peace in preparation [to face the enemy with firm-footed stability and the readiness produced by the good news]. Above all, lift up the [protective] shield of faith with which you can extinguish all the flaming arrows of the evil one. And take the helmet of salvation, and the sword of the Spirit, which is the Word of God. (Ephesians 6:13-17)

The truth of the Word of God, which Paul calls the "sword of the Spirit," may be the last piece of armor mentioned here, but I believe there is a reason for that. Did you notice Paul's description of all the other pieces of the armor? Did you realize that each piece of the armor before the sword is meant for defense and protection? God fully equips us with His divine shelter, His hand of protection, when we choose to wear those pieces of armor. The "band of truth" at our waist is built on our choice of personal integrity and moral courage. The "breastplate of righteousness" is built on our choice to surrender our hearts to Jesus and be clothed in *His* righteousness. The "gospel of peace" on our feet is built on our choice to trust in God: "You will keep in perfect peace all who trust in you" (Isaiah 26:3, NLT). That piece of armor prepares us to stand firm and ready to face the enemy when he comes knocking. And then the "shield of faith" is built on our choice to believe that God is more powerful than the enemy and able to extinguish every attempt he makes to harm us.

Finally, Paul describes the one piece of armor, the sword, that is used not mainly for defense, but for *offense*. A soldier who wields a sword has the most powerful weapon that can not only protect himself but also attack a physical enemy and do some real damage. A soldier without armor may become bruised and bloody and sustain broken bones from battle, but the sword alone is what gives him the power to take that enemy down. And that's the purpose of the Word of God:

> For the word of God is living and active and full of power [making it operative, energizing, and effective]. It is sharper than any two-edged sword, penetrating as far as the division of the soul and spirit [the completeness of a person], and of both joints and marrow [the

> deepest parts of our nature], exposing and judging the very thoughts and intentions of the heart. (Hebrews 4:12)

To begin with, the sword of the Word is what first pierces our hearts, our souls, our joints and marrow, so that we can know the sin within, seek His forgiveness, and turn our lives over to Jesus. God's Word comes alive to us, not as some simple words on a page in an old book, but as an active unlocking, emptying, and energizing path that has always been and will always be the way to know God, to obey Him, and to allow Him to change us. Psalm 119:11 says, "Your word I have treasured and stored in my heart, that I may not sin against You." We follow that path so that we can learn and choose what is honoring to Him. The more we read the Word, the more it sticks in our memories, so that if we ever find ourselves without a Bible, that Word remains in our hearts.

God's words steady, protect, and prepare us so that when the enemy does attack, we are soldiers wielding that sword of the Spirit, capable of telling the enemy the truth and defeating him where he stands. God has given us this great gift of the Bible and made it our responsibility to know it and use it "against the rulers, against the powers, against the world forces of this [present] darkness, against the spiritual forces of wickedness in the heavenly (supernatural) places." This Word is a sword ready to attack the lies of the enemy and defend our faith at every moment.

Have you ever found yourself entertaining thoughts like, "I can't do it," "I'm not good enough," "Nobody loves me," or "I'm better off dead"? Those are the enemy's lies that he whispers in our ears because he's constantly trying to deter us from fulfilling our purpose. Sometimes those thoughts become so loud and so frequent that we begin to believe them and soon give up. Sometimes those thoughts are deadly, causing many to commit suicide. That is the epitome of spiritual warfare, and that's exactly why God has given us this armor to protect ourselves in this war. We must use His Word to claim His truth over those loud, obnoxious thoughts we hear over and over again.

When I was a teenager, before I had truly given my heart to Jesus, before I knew any of His Word, I believed the lies and almost committed suicide several times. Even after I chose Jesus as Lord and Savior in college, the lies kept surfacing, but I started to speak truth over them and quiet them down. While we walk this earth, the enemy does, too, speaking lies to whoever will listen. He doesn't stop just because we have chosen to live for Jesus; we must live every day wearing the armor of God, learning the words of the Bible, and using them to conquer the enemy.

Bible study on a daily basis gives our feet a firm foundation with which to build a surefire faith, an impenetrable armor. Trials will come and go in this life, and when we face them, we can find rest in dependency on our Father in Heaven, who gave us the Bible as a guide. God the Father and the Lord Jesus have promised to walk with us in this world through the presence of the Holy Spirit. We are never abandoned to face the enemy alone. Our greatest weapons—surrender and obedience—fulfilled in our personal integrity and moral courage, allow God the opportunity to fight the battles for us. Exodus 14:14

says, "The Lord will fight for you while you [only need to]... remain calm."

## Choice Challenge

Have you ever felt the darkness of disappointment or despair? Has your heart ever lingered there for too long? Do you desire to leave the darkness behind and embrace the Light? Will you put on the full armor of God by studying the Word? Will you surrender and obey the Lord so that He can fight your battles? If these are your choices, stop for a moment and write out your decision to wear each piece of armor as you think through what that would look like for you every day. Remember how much power you have in each word you are writing; these are of the life-changing, life-giving sort if you allow them to guide your days.

## Prayer

*Dear Father, I want to be done with darkness in my life. I confess I have not guarded my heart from the schemes of the enemy. Will you please teach me from Your Word to stand up to the enemy with You at my side? Thank You for loving me so much that I never have to walk alone. In Jesus' name, Amen.*

## Choice #11 – Will You Pray?

On the final day of my fifth-grade year, I was hot and tired and kind of grumpy about it. So I made a mental wish that I could be pushed around in the wheelchair that a teacher who had just had knee surgery had decorated for a fun sports afternoon in the school fields. At the end of that same day, I was being wheeled out in that same wheelchair after I had slipped in mud and broken my left ankle. That memory speedily came to mind when I heard my fifth-grade daughter wish she'd break her arm so that all her friends could sign her cast—a month after which, she broke her arm. And not once, but twice!

If you have ever been on the wrong side of the "be careful what you wish for" equation like my daughter and me, then you know the power that words can have. The Bible says, "Death and life are in the power of the tongue, and those who love it and indulge it will eat its fruit and bear the consequences of their words" (Proverbs 18:21). With every thought that comes to mind, we have the choice whether to speak those words or not, revealing the true inner workings of our hearts. If our hearts decide to "indulge" the tongue, there can be consequences, broken bones included, even if unintended. Any form of communication infers a person-to-person relationship, where chosen words, whether written or spoken, could make or break that relationship in one way or another.

Prayer is our foundational means of communication to strengthen our relationship with God. The Word describes countless personal ways of talking to Him. A major prayer priority of all believers in Jesus is confessing our sin so that we can be forgiven, healed, and restored to our relationship with the Father. When this type of prayer is offered from a truly sorrowful heart—a heart that is honestly and wholly repentant of its "desires of the flesh" and willing to walk in God's ways—then God meets us with the ability to heal us from sin's effects: "Come and let us return [in repentance] to the Lord, for...He will heal us...He will bandage us" (Hosea 6:1). Repentance and the willingness to turn away from sin are also an act of worship and a sign that God is at work in our hearts. As we follow God, we will see evidence in our lives of that decision:

- ***New behavior:*** "So produce fruit that is consistent with repentance [demonstrating new behavior that proves a change of heart, and a conscious decision to turn away from sin]" (Matthew 3:8)
- ***New power:*** "The heartfelt and persistent prayer of a righteous man (believer) can accomplish much [when put into action and made effective by God—it is dynamic and can have tremendous power]." (James 5:16b)

That "fruit" and that "power" are evident in a life given over to God. Luckily for us, prayer doesn't have to consist of fancy words or eloquently rehearsed lines. What truly matters is the posture of our hearts as we persistently call on Him. Don't get me wrong, The Lord's Prayer in Matthew 6:9-13 is a beautiful blueprint for us to follow, but it isn't the *only* prayer we need. God wants to hear directly from our hearts. He desires depth and intimacy with each of us. He wants to have the hard conversations so that He can align our personhood with how He desires us to live.

If our lives are not in alignment with God and His will, our own desires may lead us astray; we may ask for things that are not His best for us. (*Be careful what you wish for!*) Thankfully, God can see the end from the beginning; "And He said to me, 'It is done. I am the Alpha and the Omega, the Beginning and the End. To the one who thirsts I will give [water] from the fountain of the water of life without cost'" (Revelation 21:6). God knows all things in all of time; He knows what choices everyone has made and will make. He knows what's in the deepest core of our souls, and He knows what's *really* right for us, despite our own choices. God can and will give the "water of life" to the one who thirsts for Him. Sometimes, it's just up to us to ask for it. Through spending time in prayer and reading the Bible, God can change the posture and desires of our hearts to match His. Our new posture before God in the asking can make all the difference:

- ***Asking in delight:*** "Delight yourself in the Lord, And He will give you the desires and petitions of your heart." (Psalm 37:4)
- ***Asking in confidence:*** "Jesus replied to them, 'I assure you and most solemnly say to you, if you have faith [personal trust and confidence in Me] and do not doubt or allow yourself to be drawn in two directions...whatever you ask for in prayer, believing, you will receive.'" (Matthew 21:21-22)
- ***Asking in unity:*** "If you remain in Me and My words remain in you [that is, if we are vitally united and My message lives in your heart], ask whatever you wish and it will be done for you." (John 15:7)

- ***Asking in trust:*** "For this reason I am telling you, whatever things you ask for in prayer [in accordance with God's will], believe [with confident trust] that you have received them, and they will be given to you." (Mark 11:24)
- ***Asking in boldness:*** "Until now you've not been bold enough to ask the Father for a single thing in my name, but now you can ask, and keep on asking him! And you can be sure that you'll receive what you ask for, and your joy will have no limits!" (John 16:24, TPT)

What a relief to know that God hears and answers our prayers with His absolute best in mind. That might not always bring us joy, however, if God's answer to our prayer isn't exactly what we wanted or expected. Perhaps we have prayed fervently for a loved one to be healed who wasn't, or for God to give us a spouse but He hasn't. Sometimes His answers are the opposite of our desires, or there is such delay in His answer that we become discouraged, angry, bitter, or even hopeless.

As I write this, I've been following Christ for about 30 years. I have prayed many of those prayers with unexpected answers. I prayed for 18 years before I was finally delivered from depression, so you can bet I have known hopelessness and bitterness well. I've prayed for the healing of countless friends and family members, including my father and mother-in-law, who met Jesus far too soon. I've known the question "Why?" intimately. But I've also chosen to trust God, whether He answers that question, or if He answers my prayers or not. In this one physical lifetime that we have, we may not ever know or understand God's ways, but we can trust Him that He truly knows best. After all, He is a good Father. Jesus told His disciples,

> Ask and keep on asking and it will be given to you; seek and keep on seeking and you will find; knock and keep on knocking and the door will be opened to you. For everyone who keeps on asking receives, and he who keeps on seeking finds, and to him who keeps on knocking, it will be opened. Or what man is there among you who, if his son asks for bread, will [instead] give him a stone? Or if he asks for a fish, will [instead] give him a snake? If you then, evil (sinful by nature) as you are, know how to give good and advantageous gifts to your children, how much more will your Father who is in heaven [*perfect* as He is] give what is *good* and *advantageous* to those who keep on asking Him. (Matthew 7:7-11, emphasis added)

Yes, we must ask and seek and knock; even still, what's on the other side of the door when it's opened isn't always the answer we expect. Sometimes, it's just peace with contentment. Maybe it's a form of healing or an enveloping rest from our toil. Our fragile human hearts are easily broken when things are hard, when loved ones die, when things don't go our way. But our good, good Father also sees our broken hearts and mends them. In time.

If this is a hard concept to accept, I encourage you, if possible, to watch a clip from the series *The Chosen*,[29] where Jesus explains to His disciple, "Little James," why He has not healed James' infirmity. While this scene is not derived from an actual biblical story, it is a fictional way to address this kind of broken heart and the question of "why." The actor playing Little James has actually struggled with this very question in his personal life, as he lives with cerebral palsy and scoliosis. In the scene, Jesus tells Little James that He trusts him more than the other disciples because He knows that Little James loves Him even through the pain of this life, providing a testimony to others enduring hardship, physically or otherwise, because Little James knows one day he *will* be healed, either on earth or in heaven. Jesus will provide the courage in this life that Little James needs to carry on, even if his question as to why is not answered until he steps into eternity. Watching this scene, we discover the example we are to follow: when we struggle with our pain and with our doubts and questions, we go to Jesus, tell Him what we need, and He strengthens us. That's what happens in prayer.

Prayer is that place where we can come to the Father with confidence and give Him all things that are too heavy for us to carry—every worry, every problem, every place in our beings that has lost hope. This is Jesus' specialty. He says to us: "Are you weary, carrying a heavy burden? Come to me. I will refresh your life, for I am your oasis" (Matthew 11:28, TPT). Jesus is *the* Oasis, the place where our tight chests, balled fists, panic attacks, debilitating

29 "Little James – Why Don't You Heal Me?" *The Chosen*, created by Dallas Jenkins, season 3, episode 2, Angel Studios, 2022.

phobias, and festering wounds can all be released, followed by refreshment when our burdens have been lifted. The Psalmist agrees that you should "leave all your cares and anxieties at the feet of the Lord, and measureless grace will strengthen you" (Psalm 55:22, TPT). Who better to take care of you than your perfect Champion Creator Himself?

## Choice Challenge

Are you weary? God knows your heart, knows what kind of burdens you carry, and longs for you with open arms. He is able to forgive, heal, restore, and give you rest. Will you choose to go to Him in prayer today? Will you seek and receive His forgiveness? Will you release your burdens to Him and enjoy His rest? This is a moment just for you to find a quiet place and lay your heart on His chest and talk with Him in prayer or in writing or both. Don't skip this. There is a special peace that awaits.

## Prayer

*Dear Father, I confess that I have not done things Your way or come to You in prayer with my hopes or dreams. Instead, my own human "desires of the flesh" have led me away from you. Please forgive me. I am weak and weary, and I cannot carry these burdens any longer. Will You please take them and replace them with Your rest? I believe You can and will carry them far better than I can and that You can heal and restore my heart. Call me to come close to You, my Oasis, so I can know You better. In Jesus' name, Amen.*

## Choice #12 - Will You Speak Life?

As I mentioned earlier, Jesus is called "The Word" in the Bible, so it follows that life or death can be found in the words we speak to others and ourselves. *Word* or *words* appear 1,323 times in the Amplified Bible, counting numerous scriptures that describe the specific use of words, whether positive or negative, and the effects of such usage. The book of Proverbs speaks repeatedly about how positive words can bring healing, while negative ones birth untold trouble:

- ***An encouraging word***: "Anxiety in a man's heart weighs it down, but a good (encouraging) word makes it glad." (Proverbs 12:25)
- ***A wise word***: "A soft and gentle and thoughtful answer turns away wrath, but harsh and painful and careless words stir up anger. The tongue of the wise speaks knowledge that is pleasing and acceptable, but the [babbling] mouth of fools spouts folly...The soothing tongue [speaking words that build up and encourage] is a tree of life, but a perverse tongue [speaking words that overwhelm and depress] crushes the spirit." (Proverbs 15:1-2, 4)
- ***A life-giving word***: "Nothing is more appealing than speaking beautiful, life-giving words. For they release sweetness to our souls and inner healing to our spirits." (Proverbs 16:24, TPT)
- ***A guarded word***: "He who guards his mouth and his tongue guards himself from troubles." (Proverbs 21:23)

- ***A wrong word***: "As the north wind brings a storm, saying things you shouldn't brings a storm to any relationship." (Proverbs 25:23, TPT)

Just as we must be careful what we take in with our senses to protect our thoughts, we must also do so to protect our words. Our deep self overflows into the words we choose to say (Luke 6:45), regardless of the context in which we say them. God has given us the power of words with which to build one another up, not tear one another down. The apostle Paul said it this way in Ephesians 4:29:

- ***(Amplified Bible)*** "Do not let unwholesome [foul, profane, worthless, vulgar] words ever come out of your mouth, but only such speech as is good for building up others, according to the need and the occasion, so that it will be a blessing to those who hear [you speak]."
- ***(The Passion Translation®)*** "And never let ugly or hateful words come from your mouth, but instead let your words become beautiful gifts that encourage others; do this by speaking words of grace to help them."
- ***(The Message)*** "Watch the way you talk. Let nothing foul or dirty come out of your mouth. Say only what helps, each word a gift."

There is also a right time and place for certain words to be shared, and we must rely fully on God's instructions in His Word and the Holy Spirit to guide us in this. We must not speak for the sake of speaking; Jesus told us that every word we say will be counted—"But I tell you, on the day of judgment people will have to give an accounting for every careless or useless word they speak" (Matthew 12:36). So we must continually ask ourselves, were my words soothing, sweet, helpful, uplifting, and freeing? Or were they abusive, harsh, ugly, hateful, vulgar, or painful? And when we cross the line—because, yes, we know we all do—we can come to Him with humble repentance.

God's goodness and grace are unchangeable, so He is always quick to forgive those who continue to submit to Christ. His grace is sufficient to cover our misspoken words, so when we seek Him and His forgiveness, He can work things together for good. But Jesus Himself insisted that we only speak the words that we truly mean, to not use words to talk our way out of trouble or to merely get what we want:

> And don't say anything you don't mean...You only make things worse when you lay down a smoke screen of pious talk, saying, "I'll pray for you," and never doing it, or saying, "God be with you," and not meaning it. You don't make your words true by embellishing them with religious lace. In making your speech sound more religious, it becomes less true. Just say "yes" and "no." When you manipulate words to get your own way, you go wrong. (Matthew 5:33-37, MSG)

Have you ever done that–laid down a smoke screen? Have you deliberately worn a mask around others to make them think you are something different than the person you are? Have you used words to make others think a certain way about you, a way that's not real? It's so easy to fake happiness or feign humility or wear that false face just so that someone likes you or includes you in their circle. I've been in that exact position and even put a name on it; remember my teenage nickname, "Charlie"? Well, she was anything but real. She cared too much about what other people thought of her. She acted and spoke a certain way; she used words to put others down just to prop herself up. Her masquerade was a giant mess, and all her pretending made her friendships just as fake. It was an exhausting charade.

Would you like some good news? We don't have to be that way with Jesus. He wants our true selves, not a show, not a false face, not anything but what's real and broken inside us. That's the place where Jesus meets us, heals us, restores our true selves, and gives us the *right* words to say. Jesus wants us to choose sincere words that speak life over people, over dead situations that need new life, over relationships that need restoration, over hearts that need healing or need to understand their worth in Christ. In this way, Jesus can make good on His promises to infuse that life into areas that have been dark and empty:

- ***Enjoying life:*** "For, 'the one who wants to enjoy life and see good days [good—whether apparent or not], must keep his tongue free from evil and his lips from speaking guile (treachery, deceit).'" (1 Peter 3:10)
- ***Winning favor:*** "The words of a wise man's mouth are gracious and win him a favor, but the lips of a fool consume him." (Ecclesiastes 10:12)

- ***Living thankfully:*** "Let there be no filthiness and silly talk, or coarse [obscene or vulgar] joking, because such things are not appropriate [for believers]; but instead speak of your thankfulness [to God]." (Ephesians 5:4)

More than any reason, we should choose words that worship God and thank Him for Who He is and all that He has done. These are the words that bless the Father and bless others at the same time. Even when words get away from us in the heat of an argument, we must choose to return with regret and meekness, asking Him to cleanse our tongues and continue our journey from *water* into *wine*.

## Choice Challenge

Do you struggle to keep your words from going astray? Do you believe that God wants to use your words to bless Him and bless others? Will you allow Him to cleanse your words so that He can continue to transform you into the image of Christ? He can wipe away words that were meant for evil and replace them with words that fortify. Will you choose to follow Him in thought, word, and deed? This is an opportunity for cleansing and renewing your mind and heart; beginning with repentance, seek the Lord in prayer and confess the times your words have not been honoring to God. Ask Him if there is anyone in your life whose forgiveness you need to seek for words you may have spoken to them.

## Prayer

*Dear Father, I confess that I have not always used my words to encourage others. Please forgive me, and please help me think before I speak. Please help me choose words that heal and build up, rather than harm and tear down. Please fill me afresh with the grace and love of Christ so that my words are a beautiful gift to anyone who should hear them. In Jesus' name, Amen.*

*Chapter 5*

# HOLY SPIRIT

On this next leg of our journey together, I want to help you take some important steps forward by following God's guidance, growing in your knowledge of the Holy Spirit, and grasping what grace means for your life. I've spoken about surrender, but what does that really look like in your day-to-day plan? I know when I wake up in the morning, I typically have an agenda for that day in mind. My husband and I share a calendar on our phones, so we have a basic schedule for ourselves and our kids each day. And each day I have a choice to make: will I pursue my own agenda, or will I follow God's with a willing, moldable heart and obedient attitude? It's certainly so much easier when I choose to do things His way, especially early in the day. Playing tug-of-war with God never ends my way.

The good news is that in this Christian life, we have an Advocate—the One who is able to gently take the rope out of our hands and say, "I've got this!" What a comfort to know that we have a Friend to plead our case without judgment. The Holy Spirit's job, as you'll see, is to walk by our side as Advisor, Comforter, and a resource for everything we need in order to walk in faith. And then there's grace for everything else. To know Jesus, to know the Holy Spirit, is to know grace—a breath of fresh air and space for a do-over whenever we need it. I can almost hear the Lord's voice saying, "Oh, honey, let's try that again a little differently!" It's His voice of peace leveling the stormy waves into a calm lake of refreshment, so calm that we can reflect the tranquility of a beautiful, rosy sunset as we bask in His evening glory.

By the grace of the Holy Spirit, our sun always "sets to rise again."[30]

## Choice #13 – Will You Follow?

As a new Christian and college freshman in December 1996, I attended a student missions convention called Urbana. There, among 50,000 other students, God called me into a life of ministry, caring for God's people around the world. While that calling came with excitement and confirmation of my suspicions, I gave God a few small conditions for my acceptance: *no* inner cities and *no* warzones. As the convention carried on, I met some interesting people from around the globe, listened to passionate missionaries who spoke, and heard God's whispers to my heart in times of worship. I came to the realization that I was hearing the voice of the Holy Spirit pointing me to two very specific places—New York City and Uganda—one an *inner city* and one a *warzone*! I adamantly let my fear get the best of me and told God I would NOT go.

30 Browning, Robert. "The Mermaid." *Pacchiarotto, and How He Worked in Distemper*, 1876. *Telelib*, www.telelib.com/authors/B/BrowningRobert/verse/pacchiarotto/mermaid.html

Have you ever said "no" to God like that? That was a first for me back then, but definitely not the last. And while I initially said no, the events of that week catapulted me into quite an adventurous life that has never ceased to surprise me. You see, at that convention, I heard from the Holy Spirit in very concrete ways in my own spirit, and hearing His direct communication thrilled me! BUT!! Do you know the quickest way to *stop* hearing directly from the Holy Spirit? Disobedience. So you can imagine that my biggest breakthrough came when I chose to stop saying "No!" and start saying "I'll go." Although I seemed to learn how to discern God's voice early in my faith, the obedience aspect was severely lacking. While I tended to "give in" after I resisted for a time, the blessing of God didn't flow in quite the same way as with my immediate obedience.

Saying "Yes!" to God is not normally the immediate human response. In fact, the Bible is filled with many people who struggled with this exact thing. Moses gave lots of excuses at first, Jonah stubbornly got swallowed by a whale before he finally changed his mind, and Joseph emphatically said "no" to raising the Son of God as his own until an angel came to him in a dream! So I guess you and I are in good company. As you may know, it's much easier to ignore instruction and walk our own way than it is to accept the Spirit's wisdom, do what He's asking us to do, and choose His way over our own preference, comfort, and the need to be in control.

It makes sense that as a new Christian, I didn't understand obedience in this way. Obedience comes when trust is established between us and God as Father.

Trust comes with knowing our Father as a result of time and effort on both our parts. The beauty is, when we open ourselves up and commit to such an investment, the Holy Spirit does too. Jesus said, "But when the truth-giving Spirit comes, he will unveil the reality of every truth within you" (John 16:13a, TPT). By spending time with God, the Holy Spirit begins to show us the parts of us that He wants to transform; the "truth" inside us at the beginning of our faith walk is that our human methods do not measure up to God's standards: "'For My thoughts are not your thoughts, nor are your ways My ways,' declares the Lord. 'For as the heavens are higher than the earth, so are My ways higher than your ways and My thoughts higher than your thoughts'" (Isaiah 55:8-9). Through prayer, reading the Bible, and listening to the Holy Spirit, God begins to conform our ways to His, just as Jesus turned the *water* into *wine*.

I will be the first one to tell you that I struggle with my attention span, which is one reason it took me so long to write this book. I started over many times but could not commit long enough to make a surefire dent and motivate myself further. My prayer life has also suffered greatly from this problem. It should come as no surprise that I spent the first 24 years of my Christian life "winging it" when it came to my relationship with God, and I thought that was enough. Rarely could I sit still long enough to talk to Him *and* let Him talk back. I would go through my day and sporadically say something to Him, think of Him, sing a song on the radio about Him, or maybe read a devotional book. But consistency eluded me, no matter how hard I tried.

Many people seek God only in the difficult times when He is needed most. I have often done the opposite; I seek

Him more when everything is splendid, but when adversity comes, I do everything I can on my own to find resolution, without asking God for help. I put my head down and push through whatever circumstance I am facing and not look up until it ends. We were just fair-weather friends because of *my* choice, not His. So in the past, when I needed direction in my life, of course I would ask, and He usually would oblige. Still, I would seek Him on a Sunday morning but not again for an entire week. I would get my "fill" of singing, praying, receiving communion, and greeting fellow attendees, and I'd expect all that interaction to satisfy both me and the Holy Spirit for the next seven days.

That was the *water* life—surviving from Sunday to Sunday, or for some, from Easter to Christmas to Easter again. Going through the motions of attending church only on Sundays or holidays does not really encourage a Spirit-driven life. If we want the *wine* life, if we want something different, we have to do things differently, make different choices, relate to God in a different and revolutionary way.

*Different* came for me in March 2020 when Covid-19 changed everything for everyone. When the schools shut down, the world followed suit, and I quickly hit empty, unable to get my fill on Sunday mornings. I found myself at home desperately trying to school three children, one of whom had had significant behavioral problems since age two. That child required so much of my attention that schooling the other two was next to impossible. I knew something was going to have to drastically change for *me* in order for us all to make it through the rest of that year.

At the beginning of April, after just a few weeks of home confinement, I decided to make my "quiet time" with God a daily routine. I chose to read some Bible verses and devotional material and then close my eyes, open my hands, and ask Him for help and guidance. It didn't take long to notice that when I was faithful to meet Him at the start of my day, the Holy Spirit was faithful to speak to me, fill me up, satisfy my soul, and prepare me for the day ahead. This led to me guiding my kids through family time with the Lord. We also read a devotional, sang a few worship songs, and prayed together before starting schoolwork. As I remained faithful in this, God opened my kids' hearts right in front of me. On April 16th, my two youngest children asked Jesus to come into their hearts and be their Lord and Savior.

For the last six years now, I've consistently met with God almost every day. He meets me wherever I am physically, emotionally, mentally, and spiritually. This is most definitely the *wine* life: God provides everything we need for each day and fills us with His Holy Spirit, who is always at work in us. Oswald Chambers said:

> True friendship with God...means being so intimately in touch with God that you never even need to ask Him to show you His will; you *are* God's will. And all of your commonsense decisions are actually His will for you, unless you sense a feeling of restraint brought on by a check in your spirit.[31]

31 Chambers, Oswald. "March 20." *My Utmost for His Highest.* Discovery House, 1992.

Being this intimate with God means that our spirits hear His voice, sometimes without us being conscious of it, and our will has already released our own agendas so that we can follow wherever the Holy Spirit leads that day. The "restraint brought on by a check in your spirit" refers to a specific instruction implanted in our minds and hearts by the Holy Spirit that leads us to do something outside of the norm.

The God of the Bible is a God of order, not chaos, remember? He is also outside of time; He sees the end from the beginning and knows how it's all going to come together. He says in Jeremiah 29:11 (MSG), "I know what I'm doing. I have it all planned out—plans to take care of you, not abandon you, plans to give you the future you hope for." He stands ready to help us fulfill our destinies and find the kind of future we long for. We cannot ignore Him and expect Him to bless us as we walk away from Him to do our own thing. If we ask Him for guidance and expect an answer, He will expect us to follow through with the Holy Spirit's instructions.

It is not our place to question God or His instructions. Romans 9:20 (TPT) says, "But who do you think you are to second-guess God? How could a human being molded out of clay say to the one who molded him, 'Why in the world did you make me this way?'" If we believe that God, in fact, made us and sees outside of time, then we should willingly submit to His authority out of eye-opened trust in the Holy Spirit, His perspective, and His purposes. Any kind of disregard for God or His guidance, or an assumption that we know better than He does, is sin:

> The one who practices sin [separating himself from God, and offending Him by acts of disobedience, indifference, or rebellion] is of the devil [and takes his inner character and moral values from him, not God]; for the devil has sinned and violated God's law from the beginning. The Son of God appeared for this purpose, to destroy the works of the devil. (1 John 3:8)

Jesus' life, death, and resurrection destroyed the enemy and all his power so that we can fully live our lives for the Lord and His purpose alone. "So live the rest of your earthly life no longer concerned with human desires but consumed with what brings pleasure to God" (1 Peter 4:2, TPT).

Do you remember the story of how God called us to move to Peru as missionaries? Well, about a year before that, we had some friends and their three kids move to another South American country after selling all their things first. We even bought some of their furniture, and I told my husband, "I would *never* do that!" I'm pretty sure that didn't bring pleasure to God, so He knew I wasn't done saying "no" to Him. He already knew that those three months of midnight rendezvous to work Peru things into my spirit would be necessary to take my mind out of the human-desires box, put it in the God-pleasing box, and write on my soul, "Yes, Lord, I'll obey."

We will face many forks in our roads, countless opportunities to seek and ask for the leading of the Holy Spirit to make the right decision, take the right turn, marry the right person, or move to the right place. God asks us to commit to following the leading of His Holy Spirit and learning what pleases Him—a surrendered, obedient life. When we come to one of those life-decision moments when discernment beyond our own understanding is essential, He will be right there with us: "And the Spirit of the Lord will rest on Him—the Spirit of wisdom and understanding, the Spirit of counsel and strength, the Spirit of knowledge and of the [reverential and obedient] fear of the Lord" (Isaiah 11:2).

By the way, *never* say *never* to God. He likes the challenge.

## Choice Challenge

Do you meet with God daily? Why or why not? Do you know the Holy Spirit to be consistently speaking into your life? Or do you only listen when it's easy or when it's hard? Do you desire to intimately know the Father so that He can lead, love, and bless you every day? Will you choose to make room and invest in the Holy Spirit in your routine? Make room for Him right now by writing down your decision and your plan to incorporate Him into your days. (You might get up 15 minutes earlier than usual each day to read His Word and listen for Him speaking; you might stop before meals to thank the Holy Spirit for His guidance throughout the day; or, you might go to Him in prayer before bed every night.)

## Prayer

*Holy Spirit, I confess that I have not sought You every day, but I want to, Lord. Please give me the patience and attention span to make time with You a daily priority so that my spirit can learn from and grow in You. Thank You for the love You will pour out in my life to satisfy my soul. In Jesus' name, Amen.*

## Choice #14 – Do You Know the Holy Spirit?

"They are about to have a baby!" said this little voice inside my head. I don't know where the thought came from, but being the new Christian I was, I wondered if maybe the Holy Spirit was speaking to me concerning a husband-and-wife couple I had just met. The only problem was that the wife definitely didn't *look* pregnant. We were on a weekend retreat together, and the thought persisted with a kind of urgency and authority. So when I finally got the guts up to ask, it turns out I had heard the Holy Spirit right. They were about to *adopt* a baby from overseas come Monday! However, God knew that they needed to receive restoration in their relationship from the Holy Spirit first. God used me to speak into their lives and be a part of their healing process.

That was one of my early stretching experiences being a conduit for the work of the Holy Spirit. Boldly stepping out, speaking up, being a willing vessel surrendered to His plan—none of these was my favorite or most comfortable thing to do. I was so scared at first. Meeting that couple and hearing the voice of the Holy Spirit within my own mind was so unusual, something I had never even known could happen, and I didn't know if I could trust that "still, small voice" whispering in my heart (1 Kings 19:12, AMPC). God's gentle voice sometimes sounds like a blowhorn if what He's saying requires our earnest attention or immediate action (which is where that sense of urgency and authority came from), but that doesn't always make it easier to obey. What makes it easier to obey—*trust* in God—comes only with experience. And trust comes from getting to know the

Father's heart better and better once the Holy Spirit comes to live in us by faith in Jesus:

> [Jesus said,] But when He, the Spirit of Truth, comes, He will guide you into all the truth [full and complete truth]. For He will not speak on His own initiative, but He will speak whatever He hears [from the Father—the message regarding the Son], and He will disclose to you what is to come [in the future]. He will glorify and honor Me, because He (the Holy Spirit) will take from what is Mine and will disclose it to you. (John 16:13-14)

The main purpose of the Holy Spirit is to glorify Jesus, the Son of God. The Holy Spirit is with us in all that we do while on this earth, which is why the Spanish word "con" comes to mind because it means "with," from the Latin root "cum," meaning "together, together with, in combination." We are not navigating this world alone but with the Holy Spirit. In doing so, I have found Him to operate in seven significant ways.

## Seven Methods of the Holy Spirit

### 1. He *Connects* Us to the Father.

The Holy Spirit might be a mystery in some ways, but the very core of His purpose is to connect us to the heart of the Father. Through Him, the Father calls us and chooses us to come to Him, to know Him, to realize that we are lost on our journey without Him. He is our teacher, our friend, and the speaker of wisdom to our hearts:

> [Jesus said,] I have told you these things while I am still with you. But the Helper (Comforter, Advocate, Intercessor—Counselor, Strengthener, Standby), the Holy Spirit, whom the Father will send in My name [in My place, to represent Me and act on My behalf], He will teach you all things. And He will help you remember everything that I have told you. (John 14:25-26)

Through the work of the Holy Spirit, we know the words of Christ in our hearts and begin walking with Jesus, side by side. The Holy Spirit makes this connection personal and comforting. We can trust Him to strengthen us when we are weak and advocate on our behalf before the Father when we are in need.

## 2. He *Convicts* Us of Sin.

Jesus said, "...if I go, I will send Him (the Holy Spirit) to you [to be in close fellowship with you]. And He, when He comes, will convict the world about [the guilt of] sin [and the need for a Savior], and about righteousness, and about judgment: about sin [and the true nature of it]..." (John 16:7-9). Apart from Jesus and the conviction of the Holy Spirit, we would choose sin that leads to our destruction, as is our human nature. Thankfully, His conviction, which can happen in a single moment, is what convinces us that a permanent change is needed, a lasting change that causes us to completely turn away from sin and choose life with Jesus instead. We know that "God's kindness leads [us] to repentance" (Romans 2:4). The Holy Spirit extends the compassionate nature of God, so when we look into His eyes, we do not sense judgment, but peace and forgiveness. We are introduced to grace without condemnation. Our souls are relieved of guilt and shame in exchange for joy.

### 3. He *Consoles* and Heals Our Hearts.

God's compassion is so great, so deep for each of us, that He sends His Holy Spirit into our lives to console us when we are in pain and heal our broken pieces. The Holy Spirit surrounds us with His presence, which is the fullness of God's joy, that takes away the sting of sin or the hurts of others and replaces it with peace and hope. "He heals the brokenhearted and binds up their wounds [healing their pain and comforting their sorrow]" (Psalm 147:3). And when we overflow with that joy, God is able to use us as vessels of His compassion for others, because He "comforts and encourages us in every trouble so that we will be able to comfort and encourage those who are in any kind of trouble, with the comfort with which we ourselves are comforted by God" (2 Corinthians 1:4).

### 4. He *Conforms* Us into the Image of Christ.

Jesus paid the blood price for us so that we are no longer separated from God. And then the Holy Spirit arrives on the scene to conform us into who God meant us to be, clothing us in the character of Christ, allowing us to begin our journey from *water* into *wine*:

> We can all draw close to him with the veil removed from our faces. And with no veil we all become like mirrors who brightly reflect the glory of the Lord Jesus. We are being transfigured into his very image as we move from one brighter level of glory to another.

> And this glorious transfiguration comes from the Lord, who is the Spirit. (2 Corinthians 3:18, TPT)

All the work of the Holy Spirit brings glory to God; our transformation is evidence that He lives within us, and others can see the proof of His glory, most especially in the choices we make along the journey.

### 5. He *Conceives* the Fruit of the Spirit.

Another job of the Holy Spirit is to conceive, or birth, His fruit in us. When we give Him permission to conform us, He works in our spirit to weed out the bad stuff and plant seeds that grow into the character of Jesus in this way:

> But the fruit of the Spirit [the result of His presence within us] is love [unselfish concern for others], joy, [inner] peace, patience [not the ability to wait, but how we act while waiting], kindness, goodness, faithfulness, gentleness, self-control. Against such things there is no law. If we [claim to] live by the [Holy] Spirit, we must also walk by the Spirit [with personal integrity, godly character, and moral courage—our conduct empowered by the Holy Spirit]. (Galatians 5:22-23, 25)

I am so grateful that these are not changes that *I* must *force* to happen within myself. This fruit is evidence that the Holy Spirit has entered our lives, is changing us, and is strengthening us to walk out the new life that we have in Christ. And yet another fruit of the Spirit—Hope!—makes a debut in our lives, showing us that we are a work in progress, a work which God will complete in the eternal life to come.

> Now may God, the fountain of hope, fill you to overflowing with uncontainable joy and perfect peace as you trust in him. And may the power of the Holy Spirit continually surround your life with his super-abundance until you radiate with hope! (Romans 15:13, TPT)

What joy is ours to know that joy and peace are not man-made but come from the Fountain of Hope Himself. Through the Holy Spirit, a super-abundance of hope infiltrates our day-to-day lives that is unmistakable compared to those who are without.

### 6. He *Conducts* Our Course.

Like a symphony, our lives are made up of moments in time perfectly orchestrated with others' lives and fine-tuned by the Conductor to happen in just the right tone, at just the right time, with just the right volume, perfectly intertwined to create a masterpiece—His workmanship! We may not be able to see how everything works together to make His "poetry" (Ephesians 2:10, TPT), but that alone is the job of the Conductor to put us on the right course so that everything falls into place. Priscilla Shirer writes:

> The Holy Spirit reveals God's plan to you as He orchestrates the circumstances of your life. When your spiritual eyes are open to see His divine activity on the earth and your heart is stirred to engage, this is an invitation. He has allowed you to see this "open door" as a way to personally invite you to participate with Him. You don't need to know all the details of

> how everything will work out *before* you say yes. You just say, *yes*, up front, knowing that if He's invited you to do it, He will empower you to carry it out.[32]

We may not always necessarily hear a voice inside telling us what to do, but by no means does that mean the Spirit is not at work. I deeply believe He is involved in even the slightest details, lining up our minutes with the perfect will of the Father. I also do not believe there are coincidences in the way the world sees them as random or meaningless occurrences. For example, one morning when I was bringing my son to school, a "thought" came into my mind as I was backing out of my driveway: "Someone is going to run a stop sign today." At first, I didn't think much of it, but when I came to the stop sign right in front of his school, I paused a little longer just to be sure. A split second later, a car I couldn't see sped right through the stop sign on my right and would have hit my son's side of the car had I not paused at that very moment. That God-incidence saved my son's life.

If we keep our eyes open, we will see the Holy Spirit's fingerprints on everything we do. "[We] are not [living] in the flesh [controlled by the sinful nature] but in the Spirit, if in fact the Spirit of God lives in [us] [directing and guiding us]" (Romans 8:9, pronouns modified).

## 7. He's a *Conduit* for Spiritual Gifts.

Each of us, God's unique children, is crafted meticulously for a purpose unlike any other. In order for us to walk out

32 Shirer, *Discerning the Voice of God.*

His particular plan for us, the Holy Spirit grants us gifts and talents to be used for the glory of Christ:

> Now there are [distinctive] varieties of spiritual gifts [special abilities given by the grace and extraordinary power of the Holy Spirit operating in believers], but it is the same Spirit [who grants them and empowers believers]. And there are [distinctive] varieties of ministries and service, but it is the same Lord [who is served]. And there are [distinctive] ways of working [to accomplish things], but it is the same God who produces all things in all believers [inspiring, energizing, and empowering them]. All these things [the gifts, the achievements, the abilities, the empowering] are brought about by one and the same [Holy] Spirit, distributing to each one individually just as He chooses. (1 Corinthians 12:4-6, 11)

The Holy Spirit is our source of power, but the choice to walk in surrender and obedience is still up to us. He comes willingly alongside our journey of transformation, but we must still lay down our will to do things His way. The Holy Spirit is the inspiration and energy, but we are the voice, the hands, the feet of Jesus, accomplishing His will on the earth. Our act of surrender is our form of worship of the Father, and in turn, He fills our emptiness with His Life.

## Choice Challenge

Do you sense the Holy Spirit operating in your life? If not, take time now to ask Him to reveal His work within you and around you to bring about the fulfillment of His plan for you in Christ. Do you still struggle with feeling empty or in need of guidance or direction? Will you surrender your will to the Father so that His Holy Spirit can fill you with joy and peace, energizing you to accomplish your purpose? Take a moment to write down the thoughts you have about what your purpose is and what you are willing to do to allow God to accomplish it.

## Prayer

*Dear Father, I want to be a conduit of the Holy Spirit working on behalf of Your glory. Please fill me with the joy and peace You offer as I surrender to Your will. Strengthen me to say "yes" without knowing every detail first. Help me take a leap of faith and trust You with the results. Make me more like Jesus! Give me ears to hear Your voice and eyes to see Your hand at work in my life. In Jesus' name, Amen.*

## Choice #15 – Get Grace or Give Up?

I coined a phrase as a young adult. Remember 2002? I had just graduated from college, started a new job, moved into my very first apartment, and found a new church. The church's young singles group was very appropriately named "Pivotal." Everything happening in our lives would be pivotal to the next stages of life, defined by our actions, habits, decisions, and mindsets. This would help establish patterns we'd live out for the rest of our lives.

As I carefully observed situations within this group, I noticed mistakes we often made while in fellowship with one another. Some were minor, while others were snowballing and colossal. However, these relational difficulties served as significant learning experiences; we knew within this twenty-something group that we could confront and rectify problematic issues both individually and collectively.

It was also no coincidence at that time that our church was named *Grace* Chapel. Grace—the free and unmerited favor of God—was the most significant theme in our lives. We learned to accept it, give it, abide in it—some of us for the first time in our lives. In this, I realized the importance of offering grace to my comrades on this early journey, especially as we learned how to "adult" for the first time—living on our own apart from parents, owning our first car, paying our first bills, and all that adulting stuff.

That is how "TGFT" was born: "There's Grace For That." I understood one thing, that grace needed to start between the Father and me. He freely offers grace through the gift of Jesus, and then it's up to us to accept it through the power of the Holy Spirit's work within us. And with grace, we can just be ourselves—freely, imperfectly, without fear of condemnation. Once I learned to accept His grace, I then had to learn how to extend grace to myself. This allowed the perfectionist within me to start her (unfortunately slow) demise. Being hard on myself only made me dwell in the past and linger in the pain of failure, but grace meant that I could forgive myself for the errors and try again without carrying the baggage of regret. Grace is the reminder that in His sovereignty—God's ability to see outside of time and orchestrate our path through the Holy Spirit—He can use even our missteps for His glory, even if we can't see it yet.

On this side of heaven, extending grace to one another is one of the most pressing actions that God asks of us. We love others because He first loved us; we forgive others because He first forgave us. Extending that forgiveness to others sometimes can be just as hard as extending it to ourselves. It's the work of the Holy Spirit in us that gives us the mercy and compassion needed to offer forgiveness either way. It's this offer of grace which allows us to dwell together in harmony, giving each other the space to mess up but not be cast out for the fleshly and occasionally harmful things we do. Everyone makes paramount decisions in our lives, especially when we're young. Some of these choices can carry heavy consequences, good or bad, like choosing a spouse or a career, handling money, and caring for ourselves physically, emotionally, and spiritually. If we choose now to invite the Holy Spirit into making these monumental choices, our lives will flow more smoothly and be much more blessed than if we deliberately leave Him out of the equation.

Over the last ten years, I've mentored many young women in their own pivotal time of life. *TGFT* is one of the most important lessons that I feel compelled to pass along to them and now to you. Millennials (Generation Y) and Gen-Zers are unquestionably living in a different world than my Gen-X, pre-9/11 era. Generations Alpha and Beta will undoubtedly encounter fantastical advancements while also facing the challenging, constantly changing, fully digital world. However, the truths of the gospel and the sovereignty of God remain the same, as Proverbs describes:

> Go ahead and make all the plans you want, but it's the Lord who will ultimately direct your steps. We are all in love with our own opinions, convinced they're correct. But the Lord is in the midst of us, testing and probing our every motive. Before you do anything, put your trust totally in God and not in yourself. Then every plan you make will succeed. The Lord works everything together to accomplish his purpose. (Proverbs 16:1-4a, TPT)

No matter what generation you fall under, the Father, Son, and Holy Spirit all remain the same, and all work together to "accomplish [Their] purpose" through the grace God offers us as members of His greater family.

God's grace doesn't just work in us to bring us to salvation through Jesus, to bring us under the Lordship of Jesus, and to bring us to surrender and obedience to the will of the Father. God's grace also takes all our tormenting struggles, gut-wrenching grief, and bare brokenness, along with our brilliant triumphs and exquisite joys, and works it all into His perfect plan for you and me in a more profound and magnificent way than we could have ever asked for or imagined. But this requires that we do an unambiguous spiritual trust-fall, fully expecting God to catch us when we plainly fail. This is where the Holy Spirit serves as our cushion in the midst of our failures, providing the grace to help us safely stand back up again.

> So we are convinced that every detail of our lives is continually woven together for good, for we are his lovers who have been called to fulfill his designed purpose. For he knew all about us before we were born and he destined us from the beginning to share the likeness of his Son. (Romans 8:28-29a, TPT)

When I first began writing this chapter, I remember having a big, goofy grin on my face because I have personally witnessed the beauty that only God's sovereignty can create. He knew before I was born what career path I would choose, who I would marry, who my children would be, and when my first book would finally be released into this world. None of it takes Him by surprise. Each life circumstance I endure, each choice I consciously make, each person that passes through my life—all of it is worked together for a larger purpose because I love the Lord and walk in His divine destiny for my life. His Holy Spirit conducts my steps: His eyes watch over me, His voice tells me where and when to turn, and I respond according to my spirit of surrender and obedience.

> He has made everything beautiful and appropriate in its time. He has also planted

> eternity [a sense of divine purpose] in the human heart [a mysterious longing which nothing under the sun can satisfy, except God]—yet man cannot find out (comprehend, grasp) what God has done (His overall plan) from the beginning to the end. (Ecclesiastes 3:11)

Only a truly big God, one who can see the overall picture, can piece together our individual lives for specific and divine purposes. Not only that, but He can also weave all things together into a single, stunning work of art under the blanket of His grace. Our Creator is so imaginative that He knit us each together *differently* in our mother's wombs. None of us is the same or ever repeated. I love how the scriptures talk about His greatest creation—us—and how the different translations even magnify His awesome personal nature in Ephesians 2:10 (emphasis added):

- ***(Amplified Bible)*** "For we are His ***workmanship*** [His own master work, a work of art], created in Christ Jesus [reborn from above—spiritually transformed, renewed, ready to be used] for good works, which God prepared [for us] beforehand [taking paths which He set], so that we would walk in them [living the good life which He prearranged and made ready for us]."
- ***(The Passion Translation®)*** "We have become his ***poetry***, a re-created people that will fulfill the destiny he has given each of us, for we are joined to Jesus, the Anointed One. Even before we were born, God planned in advance our destiny and the good

works we would do to fulfill it!"

- ***(New Living Translation)*** "For we are God's ***masterpiece***. He has created us anew in Christ Jesus, so we can do the *good things he planned* for us long ago."

I am giddily overwhelmed when talking about the creativity of God, who communicates passionately and vividly through His Word. I so enjoy reading various translations to get a greater sense of His meaning both in mind and heart. I, too, love to create things; I paint, do wood crafting, scrapbooking, photography, journaling, and more, in addition to my writing. Whenever I create anything, I experience immense joy as I see beauty take shape in front of me. I imagine it is just a tiny glimpse of how God felt when he created you and me. In Ephesians 2:10 above, we see this perfect example play out so beautifully in Paul's choice of words:

> Workmanship, [is the Greek word] *poiema*. Signifies that which is manufactured, a product, a design produced by an artisan. *Poiema* emphasizes God as the Master Designer, the universe as His creation (Rom. 1:20), and the redeemed believer as His new creation (Eph. 2:10). Before conversion our lives had no rhyme or reason. Conversion brought us balance, symmetry, and order. We are God's poem, His work of art.[33]

33 Hayford, Jack W. and Joseph Snider. *Prisoner of Joy: Living in Christ's Fullness and Freedom: A Study of the Prison Epistles (Ephesians, Philippians, Colossians, Philemon)*. Thomas Nelson, 1994.

I love reading the words "workmanship," "poetry," and "masterpiece." These words are not bland or impersonal by any means, for we are handcrafted by the Creator of the entire universe. What truly amazing awe and wonder He evokes with every brushstroke, like the ones we see in the sunrises or sunsets of our lives. But how much more valuable we are to Him than the rising and setting of the sun. That is why the Word also says, "Don't just listen to the Word of Truth and not respond to it, for that is the essence of self-deception. So always let his Word become like poetry written and fulfilled by your life!" (James 1:22, TPT). He wants us to let the Word itself change and transform us into the person He had in mind as He formed us so that we can fulfill His ultimate plan.

My bachelor's degree is in English Writing & Literature, for which I focused my studies and writing on Christian essay and poetry. I have never read or written anything that could ever come close to invoking the awe I feel when I read these scriptures. I especially love inhaling the Holy Spirit from *The Passion Translation*®, which specifically attempts to paraphrase scripture in a more poetic style that deeply appeals to my creative heart:

> Lord, you know everything there is to know about me.
>
> > You perceive every movement of my heart and soul, and you understand my every thought before it even enters my mind.
> >
> > You are so intimately aware of me, Lord.
> >
> > You read my heart like an open book and you know all the words I'm about to speak before I even start a sentence!

You know every step I will take before my journey even begins.

You've gone into my future to prepare the way, and in kindness you follow behind me to spare me from the harm of my past.

You have laid your hand on me!

This is just too wonderful, deep, and incomprehensible!

Your understanding of me brings me wonder and strength.

You formed my innermost being, shaping my delicate inside and my intricate outside, and wove them all together in my mother's womb.

I thank you, God, for making me so mysteriously complex!

Everything you do is marvelously breathtaking.

It simply amazes me to think about it!

How thoroughly you know me, Lord!

You even formed every bone in my body when you created me in the secret place; carefully, skillfully you shaped me from nothing to something.

You saw who you created me to be before I became me!

Before I'd ever seen the light of day, the number of days you planned for me were

> already recorded in your book. (Psalm 139:1-6, 13-16, TPT)

After reading that precious psalm, do you grasp how special you are to Him? Do you sense His fatherly heart carefully crafting you and also every circumstance you were born into? Can you feel how His skillful hands delicately fashioned your sweet infant body with a spark of excitement as you began to experience a uniquely remarkable life? His excitement then turned into a keen joy as He breathed life into your poised lungs. Your heart began to beat, and heaven rejoiced knowing that God's plan for *your* existence was and is nothing short of divine.

There is no flaw in our design, only in our own decision-making. Poor choices may lie in your past, but now you have this opportunity to receive the goodness of God as He goes into your future to prepare the way. And in His kindness, He follows behind you to spare you from the harm of your past. Allow His deep knowledge of you to bring you wisdom and strength. Allow Him to read your heart like an open book, and marvel as He knows your thoughts even before you think them. Yes, you are "mysteriously complex" by design. His relentless tenderness walks beside you as the Holy Spirit, thoroughly knowing your every word, because everything He does is incomparably breathtaking.

Once we choose Christ to govern and lead our lives by grace, God sees us as perfectly as Jesus Himself—strikingly flawless. We are forever robed in the righteousness of Christ, taking a step closer every day to an eternity with our great Creator: "And so we are transfigured much like the Messiah, our lives gradually becoming brighter and more beautiful as God enters our lives and we become like him" (2 Corinthians 3:18, MSG). This is the path of those who are seeking the transformation of *water* into *wine*, the surrendered and obedient children of God who are learning the art of choosing True Life.

## Choice Challenge

Do you smile when you think of God being at work in your life? Do you believe that the Holy Spirit can use the good, the bad, and the ugly parts of your life to make you into a masterpiece? Will you continue to walk in surrender and obedience so that He can do so by His amazing grace? Write a list of the "ugly parts" that you want to allow God to weave into something good, and seek Him in prayer for wisdom about the work He's doing through those trials. Ask the Holy Spirit to open your eyes to see His hand at work in your life if you're struggling to see it.

## Prayer

*Dear Father, You inspire me with incredible awe to think how well You know me, how exquisitely You made me, how You creatively use everything to make my life a piece of Your fine art. I want to honor You, Lord, by walking in surrender to Your will through the work of Your grace in me. Father, please give me strength not to give up, but to choose Your ways instead of my own. In Jesus' name, Amen.*

*Chapter 6*

# IDENTITY

The world has tried to define our identities from the moment we are born. Depending on what country or culture we are born into, humanity has endeavored to label us one way or another in an attempt to place us in earthly categories that inspire pride. Unfortunately, it was pride that caused the rebellious angel, Satan, to fall from heaven, eternally banished from the presence of God. Let's not take any pointers from the enemy of our souls, okay?

When it comes to who we are outside of labels, I know it may seem like all we are just the sum of our mistakes, but that is not how God sees us. We don't have to be prisoners of the past. Satan would love to keep us there—shackled by despair, walking under dark deeds of shame, feeling condemned and rejected because of all we've done.

Stop there. That is NOT WHO YOU are.

PART of who you are is the sum of all your experiences, yes, both good and bad, but that doesn't mean your identity is based on those experiences. They do serve God's purpose of creating some of your character. But on the other side of that coin is your *true identity* as a child of God.

When you surrender your life to Him, He defines the real WHO that makes you YOU.

His definition of You is this: loved, fully forgiven, chosen, redeemed, secure, completely whole, healed, wanted, free, a son or daughter of the King, more precious than rubies, friend, heir, and destined for eternal glory with Jesus.

By faith in Christ, we are accepted by God, loved exactly as we are, and freed from ALL chains of the past. Jesus has overcome the world and Satan, so we can kick Satan to the curb and choose God's freedom, the source of our life-joy. In God's freedom-life, we find our true identity and the peace that comes even in the midst of our own inner battles.

The End. God Wins. And So Do We.

## Choice #16 – True or False?

Rejection has been something I have struggled with throughout my life. I didn't really have a great deal of friends growing up. By the time I was a teenager, I was desperate for anyone's affection or attention, which contributed to a lot of my rebellious ways. High school and college were much the same, although when I went to college and committed myself to the Lord, I began to learn about my true identity in Christ. The Bible is very clear that we are loved deeply by the Father, who counts those surrendered to Him as His own children. Jesus paid the ultimate price with His life because He loved us so much. John 15:13 says, "No one has greater love [nor stronger commitment] than to lay down his own life for his friends." Because of Jesus' sacrificial love for all of us, we can know the Father's heart intimately, and He says we are worth far more than gold or precious gems.

Learning in our minds how much worth we have in God's eyes is one thing; receiving that in our hearts is often much harder to do. Many of us have experienced great rejection, even more so when it's coming from a parent or other family member, since they know us better and spend more time with us. The reason rejection hurts so much is that God made us to love and be loved! Being loved—being seen and heard—is our greatest need in this earthly life. So when that love is rescinded or purposely withheld, our hearts painfully ache with the time-old question, "Why?"

That's a question we need never ask our heavenly Father. He will never withhold love from us because He, Himself, *is love*. He cannot and will not withhold Himself from those who earnestly seek Him. "For God so [greatly] loved and dearly prized the world," Jesus said, "that He [even] gave His [One and] only begotten Son, so that whoever believes and trusts in Him [as Savior] shall not perish, but have eternal life" (John 3:16). That "eternal life" begins here and now, walking with our Savior as we learn of His love and enjoy His presence now and in the forever life to come.

Understanding who we are in Christ Jesus is the fundamental foundation on which we can build our lives, free from condemnation or judgment from anyone in this world, free to walk with Jesus in faith, hope, and love. Learning what the scripture says about us is essential to understanding our worth in God's eyes, not in the eyes of this world's culture, and especially not in the eyes of our neighbors or anyone in our lives whose opinion would try to usurp that worth. These are the truths of who we are and who we will always be:

| Old Label | New Identity | Reference | Old Label | New Identity | Reference |
|---|---|---|---|---|---|
| Lost | Found | Luke 15:24 | Anxious | Resting in God's Peace | Philippians 4:6–7 |
| Unworthy | Chosen | Ephesians 1:4 | Controlling | Surrendered | Proverbs 3:5–6 |
| Guilty | Forgiven | 1 John 1:9 | Prideful | Humble | James 4:10 |
| Ashamed | Redeemed | Isaiah 44:22 | Lonely | Never Alone | Deuteronomy 31:6 |
| Broken | Made Whole | Psalm 147:3 | Dead in Sin | Alive in Christ | Ephesians 2:4–5 |
| Rejected | Accepted | Romans 15:7 | Slave to Sin | Free Indeed | John 8:36 |
| Condemned | Free | Romans 8:1–2 | Enemy of God | Friend of God | John 15:15 |
| Defiled | Pure | Titus 2:14 | Orphan | Adopted Heir | Romans 8:15–17 |
| Addict | Overcomer | 1 John 5:4 | Weak | Strong in Him | 2 Corinthians 12:9–10 |
| Victim | Victor | Romans 8:37 | Darkness | Light | Ephesians 5:8 |
| Failure | More Than a Conqueror | Romans 8:37 | Ordinary | Chosen Vessel | 2 Timothy 2:21 |
| Outcast | Beloved Child | 1 John 3:1 | Aimless | Purposeful | Jeremiah 29:11 |
| People-Pleaser | God-Pleaser | Galatians 1:10 | Old Self | New Creation | 2 Corinthians 5:17 |
| Self-Made | God-Created | Ephesians 2:10 | Earthly-Minded | Heaven-Focused | Colossians 3:2 |
| Doubter | Believer | Mark 9:24 | Hopeless | Hope-Filled | Romans 15:13 |
| Fearful | Courageous | Joshua 1:9 | Empty | Overflowing | John 7:38 |
| Angry | Peaceful | Philippians 4:7 | Powerless | Spirit-Filled | Acts 1:8 |
| Bitter | Forgiving | Ephesians 4:32 | Unseen | Known by God | Isaiah 49:16 |

You are accepted. You are secure. You are significant. All of these scriptures above just scratch the surface of who God created you to be. If you have labeled yourself in other ways, you may need to lay those labels down at the feet of Jesus and ask for His wisdom about whether your labels are a true or false identity. Old labels might include *liar*, *thief*, *adulterer*, etc. In Christ, the labels that once defined us fall away. We are called by a new name—one spoken in love, sealed in grace, and written on His heart. The world defines people by temporary, surface-level, or self-made identities, while Jesus defines us by our eternal, redeemed identity. John wrote in Revelation 21:5, "And He who sits on the throne said, 'Behold, I am making all things new.'" The Lord Jesus is making *you* new. Today and every day, there is fresh mercy and fresh grace to *keep* creating you new.

## Choice Challenge

Until now, where have you found your worth? In your work, perhaps? As a mother or father? Or in the approval of others, trying to please others all the time? Now you know that your true worth is not in any one of these things. Your worth is in your identity as a child of God—loved, whole, redeemed, confident, free, and God's workmanship. Will you choose to believe that today? Copy down five of the truths listed above that struck you the most, starting with "(Your name) is..." followed by your new identity, then write out the associated scripture beside it.

## Prayer

*Dear Father, I have toiled for so long to win the approval of this world and all its standards. Please set me free from the shame and guilt of my past, and help me to embrace who I am in Christ. I want to live as Your child, Lord. I want to be who You say I am, to receive Your love and be confident that I am accepted, secure, and significant in Your eyes. In Jesus' name, Amen.*

## Choice #17 – Your Path or His?

Along with my earlier high school nickname "Charlie," they also called me "Zero-Brain." Nice, right? Well, you see, during my senior year, I took a left-brain versus right-brain test. Left-brained people (the analytical, methodical, logical folk) scored a negative number. Right-brained people (the creative, artistic types) scored a positive number. Can you guess how I did? Yep, I scored a zero. Apparently, being "middle-brained" is a thing! If you can function equally both analytically and creatively, you too are a "Zero-Brain." But take heart, my friend, that's just a worldly label, too, as we've just discussed. That's not what our Jesus calls you.

Whether you're left-brained, right-brained, or middle-brained, these generalized labels do not fully define who you are. You are the combination of your personality, your background, your life experiences, your genetic makeup, your culture, your language(s), your preferences, your gifts and talents, your family life, your hopes and dreams—there can never be another human being on the earth who gathers all these characteristics up into who they are in a way that replicates you. And all of these individualities within a context of faith in Jesus make you all the more unique, as now you have something within you—the Holy Spirit—to show you what you were meant to do with your unique trait collection. With the power of the Holy Spirit behind you, you can find the distinctive path that God has called *you alone* to follow, allowing for each aspect of who you are to contribute:

> Only, let each one live the life which the Lord has assigned him, and to which God has called him [for each person is unique and is

> accountable for his choices and conduct, let him walk in this way]. (1 Corinthians 7:17a)

Our lives do not begin with a clean slate. God has already assigned us multiple aspects of who we will be at birth—our DNA, our place of birth, our specific family, and our culture. As we age, we are given more freedom to choose other aspects of our lives, including whether we follow God and what He is calling us to be and do with our earthly days. Our choices differentiate us further and determine our success in walking out the life God has designed. God gives us grace for these choices, especially when we don't make the right ones, so that our *water*-to-*wine* stories continue. When we choose to walk in surrender to His will and obey His directives, He can fully orchestrate our paths in the ways He knows are best. This grace unveils to us our specific gifts and talents, making it possible for us to learn how to use them for the honor of God, the Giver of our gifts. Paul wrote:

> Since we have gifts that differ according to the grace given to us, each of us is to use them accordingly: if [someone has the gift of] prophecy, [let him speak a new message from God to His people] in proportion to the faith possessed; if service, in the act of serving; or he who teaches, in the act of teaching; or he who encourages, in the act of encouragement; he who gives, with generosity; he who leads, with diligence; he who shows mercy [in caring for others], with cheerfulness. (Romans 12:6-8)

There are several places in the Bible that discuss some of the gifts that God gives, like the above passage in the apostle Paul's letter to the Roman church. While Paul is briefly describing spiritual gifts specifically used to benefit the body of believers in community, it is obviously not an exhaustive list of all gifts and talents. I, myself, am a teacher and missionary at heart, but I also have the gift of mercy, communication, and administration. The Bible's descriptions of gifts and talents simply describe those which we should choose to use for the encouragement of the body of Christ:

> What then is the right course, believers? When you meet together, each one has a psalm, a teaching, a revelation (disclosure of special knowledge), a tongue, or an interpretation. Let everything be constructive and edifying and done for the good of all the church. (1 Corinthians 14:26)

With God's compassion extended to us, we find the freedom to work in our giftings. With the grace to make mistakes, we trust that He can work all things together for good. Nothing that happens in our lives is ever wasted when it comes to God's overall plan. He simply asks us to choose to walk in each step He shows us, even if we can't see more than one at a time. Then, when we are living out our true purpose, His favor is able to flourish fully in and around us with an unspeakable joy, just as I have in writing this book, knowing it is what He purposed me to do.

Would you like more good news? We never have to bust through doors instead of waiting for God to open them. Some doors He closes on purpose, and we can rest in trusting Him to open only the ones that need to be open. Our gifts make room for us without a need for self-promotion, boasting, or pride. Our gifts come from Him to do His will at the proper time and in the proper way. God does not require our help in orchestrating how our gifts are going to be used for His glory and in His church. Trusting Him to use us means we can *relax*, knowing that in His goodness, He guides, protects, and makes room for us.

In college, I frequently emailed a church elder, Dave, with questions about God, faith, my gifts, God's purposes, the mystery of prayer, the Holy Spirit, and on and on. In Dave's replies, he was always telling me to relax, that I didn't need to figure it all out myself or right away, that it was okay to leave some questions unanswered and just *trust* that God knew what He was doing. Dave told me to relax so often, he assigned a keyboard symbol to it—"~"—just so he didn't have to write it out anymore. Some emails just had a whole paragraph of "~" at the end.

It's okay to not have it all figured out right now, too. God's got you in the palm of His hand. And He never drops things.

## Choice Challenge

If you have never taken a spiritual gifts or strengths assessment, I suggest you pick up *StrengthsFinder 2.0* by Tom Rath and visit www.giftstest.com. This will help you understand more about who God made you to be and what He has created you to do. Are you already walking out your gifts and talents? Or have you put them aside and pursued other things? Perhaps today you hear God calling you back to your true purpose. Which path will you choose? Write about the gifts and talents you may have and offer them up to God in a surrender-prayer. He'll take it from there.

## Prayer

*Dear Father, I know that You have made me with a purpose, and I want to fulfill that purpose. Please show me the choices to make and help me be faithful to follow where You lead. I choose to walk in surrender and obedience to* ***Your*** *will, not mine. I choose to worship You alone and place You first in my heart, so You are free to direct my steps according to* ***Your*** *plan, not mine. In Jesus' name, Amen.*

# Part III
# Choosing True Life Brings Hope & Healing

This poem sat framed on my desk for many, many years, and it helped me understand that hope, healing, and beauty come at the exact time God intends.

**The Timing**
by Larry S. Clark

I have heard it said, that now and again
To know where we are, is to know where we've been
Remembering each time that God brought us through
When we in ourselves know not what to do

Today I remembered those places I've known
When I was so tempted to choose on my own
Things had not happened, as I thought they should
I cried, "God, please, help me" believing He would

My spirit was moved as a vision appeared
In silence I watched as God's message came clear

I saw myself wandering on dry, barren ground
Searching for beauty, with none to be found

I searched for someone to be my best friend
Someone to love and be true to the end
I searched through the wilderness to no avail
Broken in spirit, asking, "God, have I failed?"

Then in an instant God whispered to me
"It's not in yourself, but in Me you believe"
As God spoke these words, the wilderness changed
Beauty appeared in the time God arranged

I thank God for the vision He gave me today
Assured by His spirit, knowing this is His way
As we face life's mountains, we won't fear the climb
For all things become beautiful, when God says,
"It's time."[34]

34 Larry S. Clark, *The Timing*, poem on framed print, 1999.

## Chapter 7

# SATAN

As we talked about in the last chapter, we have an enemy who is fighting our every move. The good news is that he is not omniscient or omnipresent like God. He does not know everything, but trust me, he knows enough about you and me to injure us deeply, to keep us locked in his cage, and to steal whatever good things we are destined to receive and experience as a son or daughter of the King. He will hold one of our arms behind our backs, cripple us in every possible way, and stand in the way of our destinies if we allow it.

So, here's the bad news. It's easier to let Satan win than to fight him for what is rightfully ours. It begins in the battlefield of our minds. While Satan does not know our thoughts, he has a mighty whisper that inundates our ears with the most negative accusations, which turn into destructive self-talk. If we do not protect our thoughts, he will damage every single one, intently focusing on our flaws, our past sins, our greatest fears, our deepest regrets, and all the things we wish we could do but can't at the moment.

Okay, now, back to the best news of all: You have a Champion Redeemer who has freed you from Satan's grasp! So in the battlefield of our minds, we do not stand alone. We have the Victorious Warrior on our side who was foretold in the prophecy of Genesis 3:15, in which God says to the serpent who deceived Eve in Eden, "And I will put enmity (open hostility) between you and the woman, and between your seed (offspring) and her Seed; He shall [fatally] bruise your head, and you shall [only] bruise His heel." "Her Seed" refers to Jesus, and bruising "His heel" represents Christ's crucifixion. However, "He shall [fatally] bruise your head" refers to Christ's destruction of Satan through the power of His resurrection, through which Jesus defeated death. This is echoed throughout the Bible, in verses such as Colossians 2:15, which says, "When He had disarmed the rulers and authorities [those supernatural forces of evil operating against us], He made a public example of them [exhibiting them as captives in His triumphal procession], having triumphed over them through the cross."

Now we are armed with the truth of our salvation: the enemy can no longer have power over us...*unless we let him.* This is the choice we make daily. Will we fight with Christ to conquer the battlefield in our minds? Will we thwart Satan's plan to keep us locked in the cage of our past? Will we claim the life-joy that rightfully belongs to us and trample the enemy under our feet? When we make these right choices here and now, we find the healing and hope that Christ freely gives us, the life-joy that we are promised.

## Choice #18 – Broken or Embattled?

Frequently in my late teens and early twenties, my thoughts would spiral out of control, especially in crowds of people, and there was no way to stop the overload except to get out, to escape. Those were some of the roughest years of my life, daily falling victim to the lies of the enemy. A single bad thought would invade my soul, and that one thought could bomb my heart and color my whole day, especially if I allowed it. I didn't know any better. I didn't know that there was an ongoing spiritual battle for my mind that would steal days and weeks and months and yes, even years. Yes, I believed in Jesus, but I had no idea that the enemy was winning this battle, helping me talk myself further and further into depression to the point of wanting to die. During countless parties, get-togethers, singles' group meetings, and even dinners out with friends, I let my mind destroy my connections with others, forcing me to isolate myself in order to protect myself from what I *imagined* they thought of me. All of it, imagined and unreal. I didn't know I needed to fight our dark enemy with God's truth!

I vividly remember one particular singles' group Christmas party that I attended with my soon-to-be ex, Joe, in 2001. As soon as I walked in, the internal monologue of negativity flooded my mind, drowning me, dragging me deeper and deeper into a dark hole of doubt—doubt in myself, in Joe, in everyone there, even in God's plan. Before long, I managed to lock myself in the always-safe bathroom hideout, and then the self-defeating thoughts began to break me down as I stared through tears at the mirror:

*Why? Why do I do this to myself? No one wants me here. No one cares about me. No one likes me. This is stupid. Joe should just dump me. Why on earth would he want to be with me anyway? We should just leave. No one will miss us. This is supposed to be my favorite time of the year, but this just sucks. I have no friends. This night is just getting worse and worse. Agghhh, I want to go home! Ok, ok, compose yourself long enough to grab Joe and leave. Oh, I hope he doesn't get mad at me. He might as well just dump me tonight. I'm so stupid.*

What a waste it was to let the enemy win the battlefield of my mind that night!

We all have an internal monologue happening every moment we're awake. It is our choice what we allow our minds to dwell on. There is a spiritual war happening in the unseen, and we have armor for this warfare at our fingertips through our relationship with Christ. He has also given us instructions in the Word as to what we *can* allow our minds to dwell on:

> Be cheerful with joyous celebration in every season of life. Let your joy overflow! And let gentleness be seen in every relationship, for our Lord is ever near. Keep your thoughts continually fixed on all that is authentic and real, honorable and admirable, beautiful and respectful, pure and holy, merciful and kind. And fasten your thoughts on every glorious work of God, praising him always. (Philippians 4:4-5, 8, TPT)

My internal monologue was certainly not on a trajectory of joy at that time, but had I put on my helmet of salvation and realized just Who I belong to, I could have asked the Lord to put joy in my heart and trusted Him to protect my mind from the lies of the enemy. Dwelling on "all that is authentic and real" is a vital next step. Instead, I was imagining the thoughts of others, accusing them of not caring, but I didn't even know any of them as more than acquaintances. This voice inside my head was not the voice of God encouraging me with real truth, the truth that He Who is in me is "far greater than the one who is in the world" (1 John 4:4, TPT). I had crowded out God's voice with the one in the world, Satan, whose line of thinking was leading to death in my spirit.

In Paul's list of thoughts we should be fixed on, he uses words like "honorable and admirable,...respectful,... merciful and kind." These are words that are only reflected in relationships with others. It follows that our thoughts should be others-focused and not me-focused. The enemy would prefer we remain self-centered and prone to make choices with the assumption that we are the only important person in our world. Once again, straddling the fence can lead to great pain and even spiritual death. The Word says, "For such a person ought not to think or expect that he will receive anything [at all] from the Lord, being a double-minded man, unstable and restless in all his ways [in everything he thinks, feels, or decides]" (James 1:7-8). This is an ongoing battle; you can't just "fake it 'til you make it." If we are going to take up the armor of God and fight these battles, we should also pray for the strength to be consistent and persist in following through to victory. "We capture, like prisoners of war, every thought and insist that it bow in obedience to the Anointed One" (2 Corinthians 10:5b, TPT).

The enemy would also love to see us consumed by worry, making unnecessary decisions on the "what if" questions of life. This is an easy trap to fall victim to. So we must "Give [our] entire attention to what God is doing right now, and don't get worked up about what may or may not happen tomorrow. God will help [us] deal with whatever hard things come up when the time comes" (Matthew 6:34, MSG, pronouns modified). We find freedom from worry when we fully take Jesus at His Word.

## Choice Challenge

Can you hear your own internal monologue? Has that voice inside you led you astray a time or two? Now that you know that you can take authority over that voice, it's time to take up your armor and tell the enemy to leave your mind. Will you take your thoughts captive and choose to fix them on Christ? Write down Philippians 4:8 in your chosen translation and memorize it.

## Prayer

*Dear Father, You alone have overcome this world! Thank You for defeating the evil one so that I am not consumed by his darkness. Please help me listen only to Your Voice; help me to focus my mind on Your Truth. My mind belongs to You alone, Lord. In Jesus' name, Amen.*

## Choice #19 – Past or Present?

Joy can be a tricky thing to grasp, especially if you have never felt it before. Happiness is temporary, but joy is a lasting combination of freedom, confidence, strength, and hope that is born in a life of faith in Jesus. But it's not always an instantaneous product of giving your life to Jesus. I know this full well. As a teenager when I first gave my heart to Him, I had already struggled with depression since about age 11 and was finally diagnosed at age 14. Joy was a difficult concept to grasp as a young Christian, especially one who grew up with a physically and mentally abusive father who clouded my vision of seeing God as a loving heavenly Father. You may have grown up in a similar family, or maybe you had a great childhood. Either way, depression can still be present and overshadow your daily life. I get it.

I wish I could say depression is a matter of choice, that you could flip a switch and it would be gone. From knowing so many who have been hard-pressed by depression, that is rarely the case, especially when a chemical imbalance is involved. For me, depression lingered without reprieve for 18 long years, with waves of good times and bad times and worse times. Because of varying serotonin levels, I tried many antidepressant medications throughout those years, along with therapy and changing my diet and lifestyle—nothing was ever enough. Then in 2014-2016, after a series of tragic and crazy stressful events in our family, I was at my lowest point ever, daily contemplating suicide, daily praying for life to come to an end so I didn't have to suffer anymore.

In the summer of 2016, I found myself on a mission trip to Peru with my husband and a team of 30 people. I was miserable, thinking I had nothing to offer anyone because I myself was without hope for change. One night, the team members sat me down in the middle of them and prayed for an hour and a half until I was completely set free! The chains of my past were completely broken off me; the difference was night and day—I could breathe freely for what felt like the first time in my life. A truly remarkable transformation occurred that night, and I have thankfully never been depressed a day since.

All that to say, joy is not just a possibility for you—as a Christian, it is your new-birthright. Joy is a permanent promise of God for those who choose to follow Jesus. Joy begins today and never ends. Sometimes, we just need help releasing our past so we can freely breathe into our present and future.

A few years ago, I spoke at a women's conference entitled "Daughters of Freedom," where I talked about breaking free of our past. If you recall, it's the same choice placed before us in Deuteronomy 30:19—"I call heaven and earth as witnesses against you today, that I have set before you life and death, the blessing and the curse; therefore, you shall choose life in order that you may live." We have this choice to pursue freedom from our past or remain stuck in it; depression is like deep mud sucking us constantly back into it, being torn apart by our past and stealing our hope for the future. But depressed or not, if you are clinging to your past and unwilling to break the chains that bind you to it, joy will remain ungraspable. Like I said, I get it. Holding onto the past sometimes feels safer and more comfortable and familiar than the unknown of letting go. But we don't have to be afraid of the new or different. God's perfect love can wrap around you, shelter you, and protect you. He has already gone before you to make sure it really will be a safe and better way of life for you and your loved ones too.

Jesus referenced Isaiah 61 when He said, "The Spirit of the Lord is upon Me (the Messiah), because He has anointed Me to preach the good news to the poor. He has sent Me to announce release (pardon, forgiveness) to the captives, and recovery of sight to the blind, to set free those who are oppressed (downtrodden, bruised, crushed by tragedy), to proclaim the favorable year of the Lord [the day when salvation and the favor of God abound greatly]" (Luke 4:18-19). Jesus came to earth because He knew that humankind was and is easily oppressed by experiences we've had. Are you a prisoner of your past, or are you living joyfully in your present? I don't think anyone can truly go through life's mountains and valleys without carrying some burden from the past, but it doesn't need to continue. That was Christ's plan: to release the captives from physical and spiritual darkness so that they could breathe freely, too.

I believe the first step to understanding the bondage you may be under is to recognize that Satan wants to keep you bound and living in chains. The Bible talks a lot about the enemy because we need to be aware of his schemes, his plans, and his devices: "Therefore, submit to God. Resist the devil, and he will flee from you" (James 4:7, CSB). To resist means to withstand, strive against, or oppose in some manner. Resistance can be a defensive maneuver on our part, such as resisting or withstanding the temptation to sin. Or it can be an action we take to use an offensive weapon, like the armor of God described in Ephesians 6. It's essential that we are aware of the methods of the enemy:

- ***We wrestle against darkness***: "For our struggle is not against flesh and blood [contending only with physical opponents], but against the rulers, against the powers, against the world forces of this [present] darkness, against the spiritual forces of wickedness in the heavenly (supernatural) places. Therefore, put on the complete armor of God, so that you will be able to [successfully] resist and stand your ground in the evil day [of danger], and having done everything [that the crisis demands], to stand firm [in your place, fully prepared, immovable, victorious]." (Ephesians 6:12-13)
- ***He steals, kills, destroys:*** "The thief comes only in order to steal and kill and destroy." (John 10:10)
- ***He lies:*** "You are of your father the devil, and it is your will to practice the desires [which are characteristic] of your father. He was a murderer from the beginning, and does not stand in the truth because there is no truth in him. When he lies, he speaks what is natural to him, for he is a liar and the father of lies and half-truths." (John 8:44)
- ***He's a roaring lion:*** "Be sober [well balanced and self-disciplined], be alert and cautious at all times. That enemy of yours, the devil, prowls around like a roaring lion [fiercely hungry], seeking someone to devour." (1 Peter 5:8)

Now that we understand the enemy's plans, we cannot give him a foothold in any area of our lives. These are sneaky ways that Satan likes to enter our lives and add extra baggage to carry from our past:

- ***Sin:*** addictions, uncontrollable anger or lust, deceit, repeated behaviors/habits
- ***Trauma:*** witnessing or being a victim of violence, physical/sexual abuse/rape
- ***Generational curses:*** ancestral covenants with Satan, occult, false religions
- ***Unforgiveness:*** the failure to forgive others
- ***Controlling spirits:*** drugs, alcohol
- ***Demonic contact:*** Ouija board, seances, objects/artwork/lucky charms representing other deities, music/books/movies depicting evil acts (magic, witchcraft), fortune telling, palm reading, or speaking to a psychic.

So when we understand these inroads of the enemy, we have to make every effort to eradicate them from our lives and take basic but essential steps to leave them behind:

- ***Surrender fully to Jesus in every area of your life***—mental, emotional, physical/sexual, spiritual, and daily activities. Walk in obedience to the Word of God and allow Him to be your Lord and Savior of every area.
- ***Confess any ways you have willfully given Satan a foothold in your life.***
- ***Renounce out loud your involvement in those areas.***

- ***Take authority by the name of Jesus and command Satan to leave you and never return!***
- ***Receive a fresh outpouring of the Holy Spirit.*** Every day ask God to fill you to overflowing.

Staying free from the past takes consistent, hard work and making intentional choices, such as those we have looked at in this book. Use what you know now to focus your thoughts daily on the present and your hope for the future, allowing the past to lose its control over you.

## Choice Challenge

Do you honestly want to release your past so that you can breathe freely today? Sometimes we become all too comfortable carrying its burden that we are reluctant to let it go. Will you choose to surrender fully every area of your past and your present to Jesus? Will you resist the enemy so that he will flee from you? Will you allow the Holy Spirit to freely flow in your life with joy? Fully examine your life based on the thoughts expressed in this chapter and write a list of what you feel needs to be removed from your life. Then ask your Champion to remove them.

## Prayer

*In the name of Jesus, I take authority over the work of the enemy in my life and command him to leave me and never return! I confess my failure to sever my involvement with him and now willfully resist him and any foothold he may have had in my past. I release the pain of the past and ask You, Lord, to restore joy in my heart today and restore hope for my future. Holy Spirit, fill me afresh today and every day so that I may praise the Father freely and faithfully from now on. Amen.*

Chapter 8

# HOPE

Proverbs 29:18 (MSG) says, "If people can't see what God is doing, they stumble all over themselves; But when they attend to what he reveals, they are most blessed." It's clear that both having and following God's direction are necessary and helpful in understanding His overall plan. But sometimes we have to wait for further direction; sometimes we are hoping His direction is towards something we really want. Waiting is hard, but we keep hope alive because of God's promises. We know He has our best life in mind.

We must continue in hope with a grateful heart, not grumbling or complaining, but overflowing with thanksgiving. I know I can let my ungrateful thought life carry me away to despair if I let it, so I have to be cautious and check if my attitude is anything but gratitude.

While we wait and hope, we must also be vigilantly aware of idols that like to take the place of God. I don't mean physical statues here; I mean valuing anything more than God. It could be a person (a spouse, children), something physical (a home, wealth, things of sentimental value), or even the non-physical, like comfort, approval, or control. Even our own bodies can become an idol if we fixate too much on fitness; it's important to keep our bodies healthy as His sacred "temple," while we are sure that worshiping God comes first.

Unfortunately, I'm sure that we can agree on this point: Suffering stinks. The gospel truth, however, is that Jesus said that we would suffer, but He's overcome the world. Well, that's great and all, but that doesn't make suffering stink any less. It just gives us motivation to bear it well. And bonus—we never suffer alone. We have Him, and we have each other to pick us up when we fall and scrape our knees.

As we move forward in this journey, we must raise God to the highest place of honor in our hearts; without Him, there is no hope. For as long as we hold His hand tight and walk in pace with Him, there is a glorious hope that no man or enemy or suffering can ever take away.

## Choice #20 – Hope AND Wait?

In 2016, when I was healed from depression in Peru, the team of 30 people we traveled with was from an amazing, Spirit-uplifted church called The Prayer Room Church (TPR) in Conroe, Texas. Although we were still living in Atlanta, we visited their church once a year, and I fell in love with the Spirit of God so much more deeply with each encounter we had with that body of Christ. It was somewhat different than my church in Atlanta, and I began to ask the Lord to move our family to a church like The Prayer Room. I waited and hoped the instruction would come for five years, but the Lord did not move us from our church at the time. God had called us to that church for the previous 12 years for a purpose, and it would have been very hard to leave. Our three children were born while we attended there and loved it, too.

In 2021, however, the Lord told us to move from Atlanta to Houston, Texas, something that my husband and I had discussed for years but without any definitive plans. We arrived on Saturday, December 18th, and the next morning, we attended—you guessed it—The Prayer Room Church. And the Lord told me that day, "I didn't move you to a church *like* TPR; I wanted to move you to *TPR itself*!"

That day, the Father brought to mind the verse out of Proverbs 13:12 (TPT), which says, "When hope's dream seems to drag on and on, the delay can be depressing. But when at last your dream comes true, life's sweetness will satisfy your soul." God knew that my heart was starting to grow weary of the hoping and the waiting, and it was His will that I not have to go on hoping or waiting any longer. Joining TPR brought such intense joy to my life; it was most definitely worth the wait!

Through this experience I learned that hope and waiting go hand in hand. Our hope in this life is born out of faith in the resurrection of Jesus from the grave. His defeat of death and the enemy gives us hope that we will overcome the same as we trust in His power working within us, both in this life and in the life to come. That same power, while allowing us to know the Father, Son, and Holy Spirit, gives us hope that

> our light, momentary affliction (this slight distress of the passing hour) is ever more and more abundantly preparing and producing and achieving for us an everlasting weight of glory [beyond all measure, excessively surpassing all comparisons and all calculations, a vast and transcendent glory and blessedness never to cease!] (2 Corinthians 4:17, AMPC)

In the midst of this great hope, we are waiting for Christ's return. "Now faith brings our hopes into reality and becomes the foundation needed to acquire the things we long for. It is all the evidence required to prove what is still unseen" (Hebrews 11:1, TPT). We will not see Him return until the very end of this age; we may see signs that were foretold of the end times, but through it all, our hope carries us until then and makes His coming tangible.

While we wait for His return, we are also trusting that Christ will get us through these light and momentary troubles because they produce character—"Even in times of trouble we have a joyful confidence, knowing that our pressures will develop in us patient endurance. And patient endurance will refine our character, and proven character leads us back to hope" (Romans 5:3b-4, TPT). Through our patient waiting and persevering, the Holy Spirit refines us more and more into the person of Jesus.

As we read more of the gospels in the New Testament, we notice that Jesus, too, had to hope and wait in various stages of His life. The only mention of Jesus as a child is found in Luke 2:40-52, which describes one of probably many journeys that He made with His mother Mary and father Joseph to Jerusalem during the Passover festival. At twelve years of age, Jesus remained behind after His parents had left the city. After three days of searching, Mary and Joseph found Him in the temple, sitting among the teachers, listening and asking questions. Everyone who heard Him was astonished by His understanding. When His mother asked why He had done this, Jesus replied, "Why did you have to look for Me? Did you not know that I had to be in My Father's house?" (v. 49). The passage goes on to say, "He went down to Nazareth with them, and was continually submissive and obedient to them.... And Jesus kept increasing in wisdom and in stature, and in favor with God and men" (v. 51a, 52).

While we get no further glimpse into Jesus before He steps into His ministry years, this story tells us a great deal about Him. When we first saw Jesus in the Bible, He was just a baby; now He has grown and matured just as we did, but He is still in the care of His parents and learning carpentry from Joseph. From His question to His parents, however, we see His inner tension of wanting to step into His divine purpose while knowing that He must wait for the right time. Another translation explores it a bit further, where Jesus said, "Did you not see and know that it is necessary [as a duty] for Me to be in My Father's house and [occupied] about My Father's business?" (Luke 2:49, AMPC). He may have had the knowledge of God's purpose and the desire to dig into His Father's "business," but it did not mean He was ready to fully walk it out. More waiting—another 18 years of it—would still be necessary.

In His waiting, God continued to grow His character, and Jesus chose to trust the Lord's plan. Jesus' submission to His parents and to God wasn't resignation; it was a hopeful trust that His waiting years were not wasted years. Yes, His heart longed to be in His Father's house, but He grew, learned, listened, obeyed, and trusted the Father's timing. In His humanity, He modeled the kind of hope-filled waiting that we're called to practice—anchored in purpose, shaped by obedience, and sustained by faith.

The late Brennan Manning wrote, "Hope knows that if great trials are avoided, great deeds remain undone, and the possibility of growth into greatness of soul is aborted."[35] This has been my favorite quote for many years and a constant reminder that God has prepared great deeds for us and that "greatness of soul" awaits us as these deeds are accomplished. But "great trials" come first, which may mean a season of waiting follows as we patiently endure them and maintain our hope for all that is to come. God's timing for trials, God's timing for great deeds, and God's timing for greatness of soul are rarely according to our personally approved schedule. Just like Jesus, we are called to trust God's timing and continue in hope that He will bring His purpose to pass in our lives. Memorize Manning's quote like I did in college, and allow Him to encourage you with it through the trial days and years.

## Choice Challenge

Are you hopeful or hopeless? If you're hopeless, I get it, but it's time to reevaluate in Whom you have placed your hope. Do you choose to put your hope in Christ today? Then your hope will be firmly established. Are you waiting patiently or begrudgingly as trials pass? Choose patience as you confidently expect proven character and the day of Christ's return. Write down what you are hoping for the most in a letter to the Savior.

35 Manning, Brennan. *Abba's Child: The Cry of the Heart for Intimate Belonging*. NavPress, 1994.

## Prayer

*My Father, I confidently put my hope in You alone today, not in myself, my circumstances, or my own abilities to get through this day and all the days to come until Christ's return. I know with You, my hope is sure because You have promised to use my trials to produce proven character as You conform me into the image of Jesus. Please give me the patience I need to endure through it all. I trust You to bring all my hopes into reality at Your appointed time, and not a minute too early or too late. In Jesus' name, I pray. Amen.*

## Choice #21 – Attitude or Gratitude?

In March 2022, I was taking a short spring break beach trip with my husband and three kids. We booked it only a week in advance, so there were slim pickings. Our little three-bedroom condo overlooked the ocean directly across the street, so our view couldn't have been any better! Unfortunately, there was a lot left to be desired inside the condo itself. As soon as I walked in, my brain began cataloging its faults: tiny bedrooms, a tinier living room, no king-size bed, a wobbly kitchen table and chairs, barely working blinds, no hairdryers, only one shower, terrible water pressure, a miniscule oven and sink, and only two regular-sized towels that shed like crazy! I could have gone on and on, but the Lord said to my spirit, "See, you're not always as grateful as you thought, are ya?"

I confess, my expectations were a tad high for such a last-minute trip, and I was convicted almost immediately that I should just be grateful we could go on short notice, that Alex got that Friday off from work, that we had such a gorgeous view, that each kid had their own bed, that we could afford something this nice, that my whole family was together and having fun despite the cooler weather and everything else I complained about! Truly, God ***was SO good*** to us. We were blessed beyond measure with wonderful memory-making moments in our new Texas getaway.

This lesson in gratitude is constantly brought to mind with every trip we take for our ministry in Peru, known as Amor Real Ministries, which my husband and I founded in 2016. In Lima, we own and operate a large home called Pat's Place, a shelter we helped open in 2006 for women and children who have been victims of domestic violence in various parts of the country. Pat's Place is named in memory of Patricia Wautlet, a compassionate missionary who envisioned this home before she died of breast cancer in November 2004. Alex and I had the privilege of having her as our team leader that June on our first mission trip to Peru when we were engaged. Throughout Pat's ministry in Peru, she continually met women who were being physically, sexually, and mentally abused, usually by partners or other close family members. Alex and I assisted with the ministry at Pat's Place during our time living in Peru and eventually took over the home in 2016.

We receive pictures almost daily from Laura, the Director of Pat's Place, who takes amazing care of up to 35 women and children who can live there at any given time. She homeschooled about 20 children for two years because of Covid. Every March, the kids start a new school year with brand new uniforms, shoes, and backpacks. What amazing gratitude they have for every little thing they possess. We have never met more content, kind, and loving people than we have found in Peru over the last 22 years. They are not stingy about what they own; they go above and beyond to generously share their resources with our American teams that come on mission trips.

One of the ladies who has lived at Pat's Place the longest, Consuelo, was raised by her grandparents and uncle after her mother died when Consuelo was just six years old. They physically and mentally abused her from age 10 on, and her uncle began molesting her at age 12. She gave birth to a daughter by her uncle, and her grandparents threatened to kill her if she told anyone the truth about it. Since the Lord brought her and her daughter to Pat's Place, Consuelo's countenance has completely transformed, as God has worked in her from the inside out. Consuelo has been mostly blind her entire life, but now she receives vision treatments. She loves to sing and wants to study massage therapy so she can support herself and her daughter. She is a leader at Pat's Place and is happier than she has ever been. She is grateful for her salvation, her transformation, and every way that the Lord has blessed her and her daughter.

The residents of Pat's Place see "PAT" as an acronym; P is for "Paz" (peace), A is for "Amor" (love), and T is for "Transformacion" (transformation). They know that God is their source of peace, love, and transformation, and that He provides for their every need while living in our home. They have an abundance of food, clothing, and personal items that are constantly being donated. The children have ample toys, school supplies, and personal items as well. Christmas is the best time of the year, of course, and the children are so grateful when they get just one or two gifts!

Gratitude is essential to finding the peace of God in our lives. When we choose to move beyond a grumbling attitude into hopeful gratitude, our eyes can see everything from a different perspective, like that of the families at Pat's Place. They have been rescued from a life of lonely torment, emotional agony, and sad neglect. When they join our Pat's Place family, they receive the love of Christ, sometimes for the very first time, along with healing therapy, parental and job training, and the ability to thrive as their own family unit. Everything they need for a new life of faith, hope, and love. They worry for nothing and overflow with grateful hearts, just as Paul instructed:

> Don't be pulled in different directions or worried about a thing. Be saturated in prayer throughout each day, offering your faith-filled requests before God ***with overflowing gratitude***. Tell him every detail of your life, then God's wonderful peace that transcends human understanding, will guard your heart and mind through Jesus Christ. (Philippians 4:6-7, TPT, emphasis added)

A heart of gratitude doesn't just see a cup half-full; it sees a cup that's overflowing in our own lives so we can give generously to those around us out of our own abundance. Gratitude is not just for those of us who are "rich" by earthly standards or living such an amazing life that we can be happy all the time. God wants us to be grateful no matter what our circumstances are, and in return, He gives us lasting joy.

Paul wrote to the Thessalonians, "Be cheerful no matter what; pray all the time; thank God no matter what happens. This is the way God wants you who belong to Christ Jesus to live" (1 Thessalonians 5:16-18, MSG). Gratitude doesn't disappear in the face of adversity; instead, gratitude minimizes the size of our problems so we can patiently trust God to give us strength for battle. Allowing a sour attitude to take control can be as easy as letting the enemy lead, rather than standing up to Satan and warding him off with the Word of God. Gratitude is the incentive we have to treasure God's Word in our hearts so that we will not sin against Him. A lack of gratitude steals our hope that Christ will really take care of all our needs.

Paul also wrote to the Colossians, "*Always* be thankful" (Colossians 3:15, TPT, emphasis added). He made it clear that choosing life means choosing gratitude, not a negative attitude. When God called Alex and me to sell most of our belongings to move to Peru, I knew I had to make a significant mental shift first. Frankly, many Americans like me have a "more" mentality; we think that the one thing that will make us happy is "more" than what we have right now. During the year before our international move, I had to ask the Lord to change my thought process whenever going into a store. My "more" thinking had to become "less." I'll be honest, it was not easy. Two months before the move, we prepped for one big yard sale of everything but memorabilia, but I wasn't sure I could handle watching my once-treasures sold for peanuts. I sincerely believe God's mercy took my impending sadness out of the equation, as I was diagnosed with mononucleosis just before the big day. God's kindness kept me from having to watch it all being taken away.

Jennie Allen writes, "God made sure to include a clear call to thankfulness in Scripture because He knows that **only when we're planted in the soil of gratitude will we learn and grow and thrive.**"[36] This attitude of gratitude sets us apart, and it makes any situation we face surmountable with Jesus at our side. We may not always have the right attitude at first, but if the Holy Spirit is at

36 Allen, Jennie. *Get Out of Your Head: Stopping the Spiral of Toxic Thoughts.* WaterBrook, 2020, emphasis original.

work within us, He will plant us in the soil of gratitude when it's needed most. The true avenue of hope in our lives springs forth from a grateful heart.

## Choice Challenge

Gratitude is so critical to the direction of the Christian's mind and spirit. Your thought life influences your emotions, and your emotions can carry you away to despair. Do you have a heart of gratitude, or just plain attitude? Which would you prefer? Will you choose to be thankful in all circumstances today? Write a list of 50 things you are thankful for.

## Prayer

*Dear Father, I have not lived every day with a grateful heart; please forgive me. Please open my eyes to count my blessings so that my joy may be full. You are truly a good God, a compassionate Father, who gives generously, and I place my "more" mentality in Your capable hands. Mold me into Your grateful child as I put my hope in You alone. In Jesus' name, Amen.*

## Choice #22 – Pain or Purpose?

Once upon a time, the only surgery I had to list on medical records was having my wisdom teeth removed as a teenager. Those were the good ol' days. Fast forward to the present and a whopping ten major surgeries later, I've certainly endured my share of pain and healing alongside each one. Still, I know there are many people with much worse health conditions than what I have suffered through. I wake up every day thanking the Lord for being able to walk and to take care of my family as best I can.

> Jesus said, 'I have told you these things, so that in Me you may have [perfect] peace. In the world you have tribulation and distress and suffering, but be courageous [be confident, be undaunted, be filled with joy]; I have overcome the world.' [My conquest is accomplished, My victory abiding] (John 16:33).

Sweet victory. In Christ, we have *overcome the world.* Such a phrase sounds so fulfilling to our souls. The reality—of reality—is not quite as delicious. We all have our mountains to climb, and yet when we think of troubles around the world, the poverty, the wars, the global viruses, and so on, we gain perspective on our little molehills. That doesn't make our trials and sufferings meaningless or easy to endure. Perspective just gives us the opportunity to thank God that our situations are not worse; perspective can give us that perfect peace to be confident and undaunted in facing our difficulties.

Our final goal in this lifetime is to be able to know God intimately; He is the true prize. His blessings flow alongside such a relationship, but they are not the endgame. So when we face these trials, He wants to draw us closer to Himself, comfort us, and encourage us because He loves us so dearly. His heart of compassion woos us until we can hear His heartbeat. He allows these trials to take place because He has a plan in mind. The Message Bible puts it this way:

> You let the distress bring you to God, not drive you from him. The result was all gain, no loss. Distress that drives us to God does that. It turns us around. It gets us back in the way of salvation. We never regret that kind of pain...And now, isn't it wonderful all the ways in which this distress has goaded you closer to God? You're more alive, more concerned, more sensitive, more reverent, more human, more passionate, more responsible. Looked at from any angle, you've come out of this with purity of heart. (2 Corinthians 7:9-13, MSG)

It's easy to read these scriptures that sound so positive ("We never regret that kind of pain"), but it's really not easy at all to go through the distress that "drives us to God." I know. I really do. So hear me out, okay? For the last five years, the Lord has given me single words to focus my heart each year (renew, surrender [twice], and hope). In 2025, it wasn't just one word, but a phrase: "endurance on the wings of diligence and perseverance." It didn't take me long to realize that 2025 would include serious obstacles and that my faith would be tested in the process.

Let me paint you a picture. In January of 2025, my mother, who had just moved from Massachusetts to a Texas apartment near me the previous November, was diagnosed with her fourth cancer (after beating three other cancers in 2023). She began treatment in February, but her body didn't receive it well. She spent the first two weeks of March in the hospital following a heart attack, while also facing pneumonia, congestive heart failure, and kidney trouble. She was not able to live alone after that, so she moved in with my family, specifically into my home office, as she recovered.

Well, in January through March, I was in the middle of taking classes towards my Master's in Ministry. In February, I had two ministry trips planned while trying to bring this book to life with my publisher, eyeing a September 2025 release date. When March came, I began caring for my mother and children solo whenever Alex traveled for work or ministry, and I decided to put my degree program aside for the time being. Mom had many appointments but couldn't yet drive, so that took up much of my time. Alex and I had also been serving as youth pastors at our church for nearly two years with the hopes that our two teenage daughters would participate. Unfortunately, they gradually lost interest, although the size of the group itself kept growing.

April was more of the same, but physically I became more and more fatigued without explanation. I started a new lifestyle plan with a coach who was very sweet and supportive, but there was too much happening for me to stay focused for long. When May arrived, my health began to deteriorate quickly. While my mother was recovering well, I began seeing doctor after doctor, having test after test; issues stacked up with no clear diagnoses. Exhausted, in significant pain, and just trying to survive, I spent the summer mainly in bed in between appointments. I could no longer work on this book or take the kids to the pool. I couldn't exercise, couldn't go to camp with the youth group, couldn't even look at a computer or read. It was all too much.

The one thing I did keep doing was spending time with God, journaling what He would speak to my heart, and trusting that He had a plan. One Sunday at my church, the men's pastor and dear friend, Toy Leach, was preaching. One of the first things I heard him say was, "You don't give up. You lift your hands. You praise His name, and you trust His plan."[37]

Every day, God encouraged my heart with a scripture, a social media post, a song, a devotion, a text from a friend, and so on. So I didn't give up. And God didn't stop speaking:

- ***There's joy ahead:*** "So be truly glad. There is wonderful joy ahead, even though you must endure many trials for a little while. These trials will show that your faith is genuine. It is being tested as fire tests and purifies gold—though your faith is far more precious than mere gold. So when your faith remains strong through many trials, it will bring you much praise and glory and honor on the day when Jesus Christ is revealed to the whole world." (1 Peter 1:6-7, NLT)

37 Toy Leach, sermon at The Prayer Room Church, Conroe, TX, personal communication, April 2025.

- ***Keep your confident trust:*** "So do not throw away this confident trust in the Lord. Remember the great reward it brings you! Patient endurance is what you need now, so that you will continue to do God's will. Then you will receive all that he has promised." (Hebrews 10:35-36, NLT)
- ***Grace is sufficient:*** "He has said to me, "My grace is sufficient for you [My lovingkindness and My mercy are more than enough—always available—regardless of the situation]; for [My] power is being perfected [and is completed and shows itself most effectively] in [your] weakness." Therefore, I will all the more gladly boast in my weaknesses, so that the power of Christ [may completely enfold me and] may dwell in me." (2 Corinthians 12:9)

This year, my journal has filled up with the one most powerful thing that has meant the most to me all my life: words. God comforts me and lifts me up in the way that I need most.

Over the summer that year, my mother beat her cancer once again. Finally, in September of 2025, I was diagnosed with pre-diabetes, lupus, fibromyalgia, TMJ disorder, sleep apnea, and fatty liver disease, along with high cholesterol and high blood pressure. Treatment began while testing continued, as well as the list of issues I still faced without explanation. (At the present moment, it's October, and I have been able to steal away to a cabin for a week to work on this book. And I have the flu. So there's that, too.)

In the midst of an already long year, our family has also been enduring a family member's mental health crisis that has caused a great deal of trauma to all of us. I only add this here because the obstacles that life brings us are normal to the human plight and will continue until Christ comes back for His own. As for me, I find immense comfort in the knowledge that Jesus, too, endured so much more than I am, more than our family is, and for good purpose: "We do this by keeping our eyes on Jesus, the champion who initiates and perfects our faith. Because of the joy awaiting him, he endured the cross, disregarding its shame. Now he is seated in the place of honor beside God's throne" (Hebrews 12:2, NLT).

Jesus *endured the* ***cross***. Nothing—absolutely nothing—that I have gone through or will ever go through compares to what Jesus went through. For me. For you. For every human being that ever lived. He *endured* because of the joy of knowing that we would belong to Him, that we would be reconnected with Father God, that His sacrifice and suffering were the exact necessary ransom to pay for *our* sins.

That's true suffering.

For the joy set before me in knowing that you will one day read this book and draw closer to Father God, I will gladly endure this year of suffering, and then some.

Our problems, our pain, refine us like gold and bless us with life-joy and a more sensitive and passionate spirit within—a purity of heart, soul, and mind. Our Master longs to take us from that *water* life to the *wine* life, and sometimes that means the grapes have to be crushed and purified. So He takes our thoughts, our words, our intentions, our aspirations, our bodies, our attitudes, our relationships, our homes, our worship—and when He says, "it's time," our once-flat, basic *water* is transformed into triumphant-life *wine*. This was His plan all along.

Peter wrote to remind us that this world and all its troubles are temporary: "[You do not suffer alone.] After you have suffered for a little while, the God of all grace [who imparts His blessing and favor], who called you to His own eternal glory in Christ, will Himself complete, confirm, strengthen, and establish you [making you what you ought to be]" (1 Peter 5:9-10).

We do not suffer alone. And we do not suffer without hope. We stand together in our sufferings, hoping and knowing that they produce character while we wait for Christ to complete and strengthen us, molding us into the people He always meant for us to be. God cares so deeply about our worries and anxieties and does not abandon us in them. We choose to endure and trust that God's grace is sufficient for the battles we face. We choose in humility to walk out self-discipline and trust we are on the right path as we hold the hand of our Champion.

## Choice Challenge

Are you struggling through a trial right now? Do you need godly perspective on your suffering? Ask Jesus for His eyes to see what you're going through. Will you choose to open your heart and let Him fill you with hope? Hope in Christ will not disappoint you. Will you choose to stand firm in your faith, letting the distress drive you into the arms of your Champion? Ask your Champion Jesus to speak peace and strength to your heart for your current trials. Then stop and listen, and write down what He says.

## Prayer

*Dear Father, my distress is overwhelming at times; I cannot stand up under it. Will You hold me on this journey and strengthen me to endure? Please heal my wounds and complete the purifying work in me that You have started. Open my eyes to see my trials from Your perspective so that hope can carry me through. In Jesus' name, Amen.*

Chapter 9

# HEALING

I have heard it said many times: "Hurt people, *hurt* people." And well, we've all been hurt, right? So now's your chance to open those wounds a little, let God have a peek inside, and give Him space to do what He does best—heal your heart. That's how He—and you—can change the world. Because healed people bring the hurt people to the Healer.

True life and beauty flow from healed hearts. And no doubt, the world and the enemy will do their very best to hurt your heart again, try to tear you away from the Healer so you can go back to your hurting ways. You may find that it's often people from within the church who will be the culprit because we spend considerable time in a church fellowship and are less likely to guard our hearts the way we might with nonbelievers. We are more trusting, more open and revealing, less likely to expect betrayal. And rightly so; we hope for the best out of our brothers and sisters in the church. But yes, my friend, it is an unfortunate reality that we are imperfect people relating imperfectly. So we are called to use the tools God gives us in His Word to learn how to deal with these offenses with grace.

Rejection is one of the worst hurts we can experience, especially when it's coming from a close family member or friend. Just remember that your worth is not based on their opinion but on the truth of God. Learning what the Bible says about us is pivotal to understanding how much we are valued by God.

Ultimately, Satan is out to destroy our hearts and our peace, so he likes to cause pain and fear whenever he gets the chance. Healing, peace, and hope are only found in one place: the arms of Jesus. Let that be our aim.

## Choice #23 – Fraught or Free?

It troubles me so much to know that there are countless people all over the world hurting so deeply and don't see a way out of the pit of depression. My empathy for all those who suffer flows from the hope of healing for all of them because I know what the Bible says. Our compassionate Father in heaven has a singular theme, this one statement we can all cling to in this situation: "Thus says the Lord, the God of David your father (ancestor): 'I have heard your prayer, I have seen your tears. Behold, I am healing you'" (2 Kings 20:5). God is not some far-away ruler who just tells us what to do. He flows with endless mercy. He's relentlessly tenderhearted and warmly understanding of our pain.

God loves us so much that in Isaiah 49:16 (NLT), He says, "See, I have written your name on the palms of my hands." There's a story in Jewish tradition that's part of the Talmud, which explains this verse. It speaks of Israel as God's daughter who asks Him to "Put me like a seal on your heart, Like a seal on your arm" (Song of Solomon 8:6). In the story, God explains that since those places—His heart and arm—aren't always visible, He chooses instead to inscribe her name on the palms of His hands.[38] God has written our names on His palms as well, so He is constantly reminded of us, ready to take action when we are hurting or feeling helpless and alone. However, His response to our pain isn't always immediate healing, but it's not because we aren't seeking Him enough or not praying enough or anything else we are or are not doing. Sometimes His answer is simply to wait on Him.

Are you suffering today? I want you to know I feel your pain deeply. As I mentioned earlier, after 18 years of suffering, I had a very miraculous "deliverance" experience which instantly freed me from the darkness of depression in 2016. While this type of sensational overnight healing can happen, I know that depression can also go on for many years without any significant changes, as it did for me and does for so many. I firmly believe that medication is sometimes necessary to help regulate various chemicals in the body that contribute to this condition; there is *no* shame in this. Also, having a supportive environment, being surrounded by loving people, is also of grave importance. Suffering in the silence of isolation only leads to a deeper darkness of soul.

Depression is not a choice; it's a battle that takes place in the body, soul, and spirit, and the weapons we can actively choose for waging this war are essential for triumph over this shadow enemy. Following my deliverance, the Lord

38 *Taanit* 4a:14. *Sefaria*, https://www.sefaria.org/Taanit.4a.14?lang=bi. Accessed 12 Feb. 2026.

imparted to me several critical directives to utilize to keep depression from returning. They are also important choices we can make even while still suffering from depression that may help lift us out of the miry pit. I call them the "Seven Asks."

## ASK #1: Ask God for Forgiveness

Matthew 3:2 says, "Repent [change your inner self—your old way of thinking, regret past sins, live your life in a way that proves repentance; seek God's purpose for your life], for the kingdom of heaven is at hand." Often, our spirits become weighed down because we carry the guilt of our own sin. But living as a follower of Jesus, we do not have to carry that burden any longer. The act of confessing our sins is the beginning of healing from the shame and guilt associated with them. This is a conscious act of our will, not a natural tendency, and sometimes harder than we think:

> Though repentance can seem like a hard thing to do—something we dread—the result of true repentance is neither shame nor depression but a sense of lightness, relief and joy. The sins that once burdened us are lifted by the grace of God. Repentance frees us so we can bask in his mercy rather than wallow in our sin. Though it's good to experience godly sorrow, the ultimate result of repentance is peace.[39]

39 Spangler, Ann. "Day 82." *Experiencing the Greatness of God*. Christian Art Publishers, 2020.

Such relief is a step in the right direction for those of us who struggle with depression. There is joy on the other side of repentance, but it's still just the beginning.

### ASK #2: Ask God to Help You Forgive

Ephesians 4:32 says, "Be kind and helpful to one another, tender-hearted [compassionate, understanding], forgiving one another [readily and freely], just as God in Christ also forgave you." Forgiving others is absolutely one of the hardest steps to take in the direction of freedom, but oh-so essential. When we choose to forgive someone, we are surrendering the anger, bitterness, and resentment that may have been holding *us* captive. In truth, sometimes it takes more than just one choice to forgive, if we hang onto any of those gut-punch emotions. It may be necessary to forgive *and keep on forgiving* someone until the Holy Spirit removes the burden entirely from our shoulders. Whether or not that someone is sorrowful for their sin against us, we still must choose to release the pain they have caused us. Scripture commands us to follow this step because it frees us once again to joy, hope, and peace.

### ASK #3: Ask for Help

This step is twofold: we should ask God for help first, then seek help from others. God is readily available to hear our prayers every moment of every day, and we know that He is perfectly capable of healing. He may not do what we want Him to do right when we want Him to do it, but He never dismisses the longings of our hearts. Psalm 40:1-3a says:

> I waited patiently and expectantly for the Lord; and He inclined to me and heard my cry. He brought me up out of a horrible pit

> [of tumult and of destruction], out of the miry clay, and He set my feet upon a rock, steadying my footsteps and establishing my path. He put a new song in my mouth, a song of praise to our God.

Whether we wait a day, a month, a year, 18 years—He will answer our prayers! The key is to wait on Him, and He will send His Holy Spirit to lift us up. He is a good God, a loving Father, and our tears matter to His heart:

- ***He answers and delivers:*** "I sought the Lord [on the authority of His word], and He answered me, and delivered me from all my fears." (Psalm 34:4)
- ***He hears and restores:*** "God, my God, I yelled for help and you put me together. God, you pulled me out of the grave, gave me another chance at life when I was down-and-out." (Psalm 30:2, MSG)

God also equips us with resources in other people to help us through the healing process. This may look like a psychiatrist, psychologist, counselor, or friend who is there to talk through things, answer questions, and direct our thought processes. This, too, is not a quick fix, but talk therapy can easily relieve us of carrying unnecessary baggage from our past and help us walk confidently into the future without that pain. Proverbs 27:9 says, "Oil and perfume make the heart glad; so does the sweetness of a friend's counsel that comes from the heart."

## ASK #4: Ask God for Faithful Friends

Isolating ourselves is how the enemy works his will the best. When we are disconnected from truth-sharing friends or a loving community that can help us recognize the enemy's attacks, our depression can linger longer than perhaps necessary. Ecclesiastes 4:9-12 says:

> Two are better than one because they have a more satisfying return for their labor; for if either of them falls, the one will lift up his companion. But woe to him who is alone when he falls and does not have another to lift him up. Again, if two lie down together, then they keep warm; but how can one be warm alone? And though one can overpower him who is alone, two can resist him. A cord of three strands is not quickly broken.

The Lord has called us to operate within a church community. We are to "do life" together, not apart from one another. In this way, we share one another's burdens; we mourn together; we celebrate together; we pray together. Begin by asking the Lord to bring you strong and faithful friends who will stick "closer than a brother" (Proverbs 18:24).

### ASK #5: Ask God for a Heart of Gratitude

As we saw earlier, an ungrateful heart drags us down and causes us to remain in a state of restlessness. We are unable to see the many blessings surrounding us if we find nothing to be thankful for. We cannot receive the comfort the Lord offers because we are too consumed by what we lack. Worrying is the result of this restlessness because we are unsure that our needs will ever be met. Yet the God of the Scriptures proves time and again within the Word that He is trustworthy, faithful, and more than able to provide all that we need, and more so. That is why the apostle Paul gives us this instruction:

> Do not be anxious or worried about anything, but in everything [every circumstance and situation] by prayer and petition ***with thanksgiving***, continue to make your [specific] requests known to God. And the peace of God [that peace which reassures the heart, that peace] which transcends all understanding, [that peace which] stands guard over your hearts and your minds in Christ Jesus [is yours]. (Philippians 4:6-7, emphasis added)

The peace of God is contingent on the thanksgiving we offer to the Lord in prayer. Ask God to open your eyes to see the blessings around you, and His peace will not be far behind.

### ASK #6: Ask the Holy Spirit to Renew Your Mind

Another critical step towards freedom from depression is allowing the Holy Spirit access to our minds. What we choose to dwell on in our thoughts greatly affects our actions and emotions. In order to move beyond our current emotional circumstances, we must allow our thought patterns to be transformed into those of Jesus so we can also spiritually mature into the person we are meant to be:

> And do not be conformed to this world [any longer with its superficial values and customs], but be transformed and progressively changed [as you mature spiritually] by the ***renewing of your mind*** [focusing on godly

> values and ethical attitudes], so that you may prove [for yourselves] what the will of God is, that which is good and acceptable and perfect [in His plan and purpose for you]. (Romans 12:2, emphasis added)

This kind of progressive transformation is a work of the Holy Spirit within us, if given permission. Choosing to allow Him to do His work is vital if we are serious about finding the healing that He offers. Choosing to read the Word of God will fill your mind with healing truth and crowd out what doesn't belong there.

### ASK #7: Ask How to Be Jesus' Hands and Feet

Galatians 5:13 says, "For you, my brothers, were called to freedom; only do not let your freedom become an opportunity for the sinful nature (worldliness, selfishness), but through love serve and seek the best for one another." God emphasizes throughout the Bible that we are to love and serve one another. Serving is not an afterthought. Serving others may be difficult when we feel like we have nothing to offer. Yet loving others means that we put their needs before our own, despite how we feel or what our circumstances are. We can ask the Lord for wisdom on how we can serve others physically, even in our spiritually depleted state. God blesses our efforts with His healing touch and His favor when we fulfill His greatest commandment. Loving others is also how we show our love for Him. There are countless ways to do this, anywhere from making someone a meal to going on a foreign mission trip. It's not about the words you say but the sacrificial actions you do to serve someone who can't pay you back.

## Choice Challenge

Each of the "Seven Asks" is a choice. You may be in a place where you think there is no way out of the depression you feel consumed by. God knows your heart already. You are safe in *His* heart. Surrounded by His safety net, will you choose to "ask" for these things so that He can begin to lighten your load? If you are among the hurting right now, write out how you will fulfill each "ask." Then let His grace lead you as you follow through.

## Prayer

*Dear Father, I'm a wreck, and I can't see beyond this side of depression. I know You can see the end from the beginning; You know my way out. Lord, please lead me; guide my heart to "ask" for healing and wholeness. Please give me the strength to wait on You and to walk in these choices until Your healing comes. In Jesus' name, Amen.*

## Choice #24 – Bitter or Better?

Years ago, I met one of my former neighbors, Aubrey, who lived four houses down the street. We hit it off right away and had so much in common. After some isolated years, I was so grateful for the gift of her friendship. The Lord really put it on my heart to try to encourage her as much as possible, to support her in various ways, including meeting weekly, praying for her, and reading a book with her that I'd previously studied and discussing it. After we finished the first book, we agreed on a second book to read together, which I gladly gifted her a copy of. We had Aubrey and her husband over for dinner and enjoyed some game nights. Her son was close in age to my kids, so they often played together, too. She and I did a handful of other fun activities together, including running a local 5K race. We genuinely seemed to mutually enjoy each other's company.

Then suddenly, she started canceling our weekly meetings at the last minute. That happened a handful of times before there was just an unspoken understanding that we wouldn't be meeting anymore. After about eight months of meeting, just like that, our friendship as I knew it was over. I would still see her every now and then at our kids' bus stop or sitting in driveways of other neighborhood ladies that lived further down our street; she had introduced me to them once but never invited me to join their activities. She'd walk her dogs by my house every day and say hi. Once or twice we held a conversation, but it was never more than small talk.

The end of our "friendship" left me baffled. *Did I say or do something wrong?* I wondered. I even tried asking her during one of her moments passing by my house; she assured me that I had done nothing to offend her. *What then, did her group not want me around? Was there something wrong with me? Did she just not like me anymore?* These questions certainly had my thought life in a tizzy. I struggled with the hurt I would feel just driving by her house, or when I'd see social media posts of her and those other neighborhood ladies going out together. The feelings of being left out, uninvited, unwanted, rejected—they would rise to the surface just seeing any of her family members.

One day, the Lord spoke very clearly to my heart when I found my thoughts going down that dejected road. He said, "Your worth is not determined by Aubrey's opinion of you. Your worth is determined by Me and who I say you are. Your worth is not determined by others' rejection of you. Your worth is found in the beautiful daughter I made you to be." God went on to tell me that He had removed Aubrey and the other neighborhood ladies from my life at that particular time for a reason. He no longer wanted them to influence me in a negative way, which I understood perfectly. And just like that, a word from the Father removed the sting of the pain I had felt from this situation.

Living in community is never guaranteed to be easy. When you have imperfect people interacting in imperfect ways, hurt is inevitable. Even worse, people who are hurt tend to hurt other people, whether intentionally or unintentionally. Depression can be the result of unhealed hurts from those imperfect relationships. If we hold all that pain in and refuse to ask for help, the pain can domino into so many other people's lives; sometimes the ramifications can unexpectedly explode, or sadly, even implode.

When we come to the point of surrender before our Lord, when we release our tight grip on our own hearts, that's when Jesus is able to hold our hearts and begin the healing process. If we don't release our hearts to Him, He cannot restore us properly. Yet that is His heart for us, that He might bind up our wounds so we can find peace in all our relationships. He also desires that we can help others heal, too, through compassion and empathy:

> Now, this is the goal: to live in harmony with one another and demonstrate affectionate love, sympathy, and kindness toward other believers. Let humility describe who you are as you dearly love one another. Never retaliate when someone treats you wrongly, nor insult those who insult you, but instead, respond by speaking a blessing over them—because a blessing is what God promised to give you. For the Scriptures tell us: Whoever wants to embrace true life and find beauty in each day must stop speaking evil, hurtful words and never deceive in what they say. Always turn from what is wrong and cultivate what is good; eagerly pursue peace in every relationship, making it your prize. (1 Peter 3:8-11, TPT)

It is unfortunate that my husband and I have dealt with two churches since we've been married that have pushed us away through no fault of our own. Both of those churches had unhealthy leadership structures at the time. One of those churches was forced to close its doors less than two years later, while the other wrongly grouped us with former members who had sinned egregiously against their body. In both cases, many important friendships we had in their congregations ended abruptly, and we were devastated. However, we took God's Word to heart and didn't retaliate, insult them, or speak evil about them.

While we recognized the error of their ways, we knew that we could not "be the first to throw a stone" (John 8:7, ESV). This is a reference to a story that describes a young woman caught in the act of adultery, and the Jewish law at the time stated they should stone such a sinner to death. But Jesus told the people to let the "one without sin" cast the first stone. The people left one by one realizing that they all had sinned in some way themselves.

The truth is that we all have sinned in some way, but we are not to judge others for their sins. Jesus said, "Do not judge and criticize and condemn [others unfairly with an attitude of self-righteous superiority as though assuming the office of a judge], so that you will not be judged [unfairly]" (Matthew 7:1). It is not our place to harp on the sins of others when we know we are just as sinful. Instead, we are to "search for peace (harmony; undisturbedness from fears, agitating passions, and moral conflicts) and seek it eagerly. [Do not merely desire peaceful relations with God, with your fellowmen, and with yourself, but pursue, go after them!]" (1 Peter 3:11, AMPC). We are called to live in peace and trust that God remains in control of every situation we encounter. We believe He will make things right and heal our hearts.

Healed hearts are then able to "embrace true life and find beauty in each day" because they have released the anger, bitterness, and hurt that others have caused (1 Peter 3:10, TPT). "But what comes out of your mouth reveals the core of your heart" (Matthew 15:18a, TPT). We must also be careful to guard what we allow into our hearts by way of our senses—what we see, what we hear, what we accept into the core of our being, sometimes without really knowing it. In order to "cultivate what is good" in our lives and the lives of others, we must make conscious choices that lead to life and blessing:

> You are always and dearly loved by God! So robe yourself with virtues of God , since you have been divinely chosen to be holy. Be merciful as you endeavor to understand others, and be compassionate, showing kindness toward all. Be gentle and humble, unoffendable in your patience with others. Tolerate the weaknesses of those in the family of faith, forgiving one another in the same way you have been graciously forgiven by Jesus Christ. If you find fault with someone, release this same gift of forgiveness to them. For love is supreme and must flow through each of these virtues. Love becomes the mark of true maturity. (Colossians 3:12-14, TPT)

By the grace of God, we can come to understand the depth of sin we have in our own lives and how desperately we need the Savior to forgive us. When we realize the immensity of our own depravity, how much sin His blood covered, we can more quickly forgive the sins of others against us. The Lord left us additional instructions for how we are to approach someone who has hurt us. “If your fellow believer sins against you, you must go to that one privately and attempt to resolve the matter. If he responds, your relationship is restored” (Matthew 18:15, TPT). You can read further instructions in the rest of Matthew 18.

So if we, by the grace of God, are forgiven much, then we, by the grace of God, can forgive much. Love as the mark of maturity must be merciful, understanding, compassionate, kind, unoffendable, patient, and tolerant. Yet all of these things take an enormous amount of humility through our choice of life, a choice in His truth, a choice in each and every relationship.

## Choice Challenge

Are there hurts within you that you have tried to hide, dismiss, or forget about? Are there any individuals in your life who need grace and forgiveness? Do you want a huge weight lifted from your shoulders and are you ready to humbly forgive? This is your moment to choose to let go, let God have your hurts, let Jesus have your heart to heal. Go to Him, now. Write those hurts on paper that you can crumple up and throw away, or allow them to lead you to those that it’s time to address. And remember, TGFT.

## Prayer

*Dear Father, I ache with the struggle of unforgiveness in my heart. Will you help me forgive others as You have forgiven me? I don't want to carry this burden any longer. Help me be free of these hurts; let Your grace be a balm for my soul and my forgiveness a balm for others. Open my eyes to see any areas of hurt where grace needs to flow. Thank You, Lord, for forgiving my sins. In Jesus' name, Amen.*

## Choice #25 – Fear or Faith?

Fear is defined as an unpleasant emotion caused by the belief that someone or something is dangerous, likely to cause pain, or a threat. Our fears take many forms throughout our lives, sometimes arising in patterns that we can't shake. Anxiety disorders are the most common mental health concern globally, most commonly in women, and I am no exception. I don't think I realized how much anxiety I had growing up, but it greatly amplified when I became a wife, then a mother. And guess who is deviously happy about that? The enemy of our souls!

Some of Satan's most devilishly subtle whispers in our ears concern the loss of people we hold most dear. If he can cause us to focus on that fear, he stealthily drains our trust in a good, loving, heavenly Father who does *not* cause evil in the world but is still and always in control. That same sovereign God also never leaves us or forsakes us; He walks beside us through difficult times, most especially tragedies, loss, and grief, and ultimately heals, restores, and gives us hope for an eternity with Him and our loved ones.

"The Day My Husband *Didn't* Die" was the name of the blog post below that I wrote about fear in 2013. It described this irrational fear that the enemy instilled in my soul so deeply at age 17 that every day that followed began and ended with the expectation that God would rob me of my future husband, similar to the movie "Up Close and Personal,"[40] which I saw in a theater that year. It is a fear

40 *Up Close and Personal*. Directed by Jon Avnet, performances by Robert Redford and Michelle Pfeiffer, Buena Vista Pictures, 1996.

that Satan likes to regurgitate whenever Alex drives away or travels, and I have to diligently choose to tell Satan off.

---

I had been waiting for him to die. Since I was 17, I had been waiting. I didn't even meet Alex until I was 24, but something in me just knew—it wouldn't be long.

This gut-level expectation made more sense when I first heard that my husband's father and grandfathers had already passed away before we met. Alex recently made a passing comment about how the men in his family don't live long. So I must be right. Any day now, while he's anywhere out of sight, I could get that phone call or hear a knock at the door with the news. And since I had been expecting it, it should be easier. At least that's what I keep telling myself. I'm ready. Just waiting. Waiting.

~

A transformed Tally Atwater (Michelle Pfeiffer) stands beside the timeless Warren Justice (Robert Redford) at the edge of an escalator, their polite smiles hiding tired, taut knots—hers, of letting go, and his, of longing to leap without looking. Just before Warren steps on, Tally reluctantly places his tied adventure boots around his neck and sends him on his way. Days later, she and her colleagues are celebrating her newest promotion; suddenly, a newsbreak flashes video broadcasting from adventure-land. While bullets fire in the video's background, Tally's eyes are drawn to those boots motionless on the ground. She knows who they belong to. And her life is forever changed by the story now untold.

~

I first saw the movie "Up Close and Personal" in March 1996. The past-tense, sentimental saga of Celine Dion's song, "Because You Loved Me," echoed in my ears as I left the theater. I couldn't stop crying. Not just because of the movie's tragic ending. But because I was convinced it was going to happen to me.

What a completely senseless notion for a 17-year-old, just about to dart out of my parents' home to begin my own dash and dance, plus search for the junior Robert Redford. Why believe this eerie internal whisper that my future husband's fate would arrive sooner and sadder than most? But I did. And I never told anyone.

Just months later, three separate summer events convicted my heart with an irrefutable faith in Jesus Christ. As I began college, I also began a journey of knowing and being known by Christ, a process of transformation in mind, body, and spirit. This journey also began with this earlier unspoken lie, breathed into my spirit by a sober, deliberate enemy who simply desired to plant a seed.

Just as long as God has been walking beside me, seen every tear, heard every spoken prayer—so has the enemy, also constantly at work, "going to and fro on the earth... walking up and down on it" (Job 1:7), scheming to "steal and kill and destroy" (John 10:10). It was the enemy that struck first, soiling my open spirit with premature grief, embedding roots of distrust and bitterness towards a Savior I did not yet know. As I learned and lived a life of faith, the enemy all but forced me into a corner: If I were to truly believe that this God was in control and that He would take away my husband as fast as He would give him to me, then how could I fully trust Him with all that I hold dear? Seeds of distrust slowly grew into massive cynicism. All I could do...was live in fear. Fear that everything would be taken away.

This past weekend, Alex drove off to Savannah for a Boys' Weekend. I was so unconsciously angry that he chose to leave me and our two daughters that the stealthy self-sabotage sprite set in, tagging along its faithful twins of procrastination and the munchies. Eating chocolate-covered almonds, I sat weeping while watching a Hallmark channel second-chance romance about a young widower and his two children.

Weeping. Like that night, half my life ago. And suddenly that whisper. "It's going to happen to me."

Then a louder whisper: "It's a lie."

Finally, the truth. The Truth, now filling my heart, reminded me that He has set me free from the chains of the enemy, that Jesus shines light into the darkness of all of Satan's lies—and I no longer have to live in fear or believe in a vindictive, terrifying God who wants only to bring me pain and despair. I can know and be known by a loving Father, who may give and take away, but in His sovereignty, works it all together for good because He has called me to walk in His purposes, His practices, His possibilities.

This God of relentless tenderness knows, too, that the enemy's scheming lies run deep within me. Only His mercy can uproot it all and replant His Word of truth and life—His mountain-moving, richly reviving grace that will allow me to leave behind the fatalist, naïve little girl and become the woman of faith I am meant to be.

---

**"When I am afraid, I will trust in you. Psalm 56:3. Psalm 56:3."**

No, that's not a typo. Those are lyrics to a basic tune I came up with when I was teaching children songs in a vacation Bible school during my 1999 mission trip to New York City. Psalm 56:3 was one of our memory verses. It came to mind in 2020 when having my own children memorize Bible verses, and they found the tune catchy. Of all the verses they learned that year, this is the one that sticks in their minds because of that tune. I'm glad because that verse will definitely come in handy as they grow up.

For me, fear has long been one of those devouring lies of the enemy and was birthed in me at a young age. Fear for my physical safety. Fear of rejection, failure, and being alone, (Fear of missing out FOMO!) The struggle is real!, of being left behind, of losing control. It's hard to pinpoint one of them as the overarching fear of my childhood; they all took a major toll that caused me to grow up faster than most. In eighth grade, I was voted "Most Serious" by my classmates. Oddly enough, my brother earned the same vote the previous year. Perhaps fear made us both more self-aware than most kids our age. I know I had to conjure ways of defending myself against the enemy and the strength to do it. Most of the time I just let him win; I didn't see a point to fighting. I allowed fear to tear me apart from the inside out.

Fear for my physical, emotional, and mental safety at home shook me up all the way through my senior year of high school. The bathroom was my safe place because it was the only room in the house with a lock on the door. So whenever Dad would come after me, I would run in there as fast as I could. That didn't stop him from yelling at me from outside it, demanding I open the door and face my impending corporal punishment. And then there were the nights after dinner when my parents stayed at the table talking about me, not realizing I was sitting on the stairs around the corner, hidden and listening. Dad would go on about all the things that were wrong with me. I usually just sat there and cried, but sometimes I would get so angry, run around the corner, and start defending myself, only to be chased into the bathroom again.

Thank goodness I survived childhood, although I took most of that fear along with me into young adulthood. Fear of rejection crowded my thought life in college; making friends as a baby Christian did not come easily. My fear of abandonment was fueled when Dad once forgot to pick me up for a school break. The fear of failure tormented me as I tried to keep up in my math classes. I still have dreams that I've fallen behind or that I'm going into a test completely unprepared. Actually, my only C grade in college came in my Anglo-Saxon Literature course because I neglected to write a paper. Sadly, it was the one-tenth of a point in my GPA that kept me from being Magna Cum Laude. I had to settle for Cum Laude. (Oh, the horror!)

Fear of rejection would have to be the longest-running terrorizer in my corner. I have struggled with my weight my entire life, so my own self-rejection busts out with every glance in the mirror. Too often, I still let it creep in if I don't catch my thoughts in time to kick 'em out. I have learned that fears are only powerful if we feed them, but if we fiercely defend our minds with the strength of Christ, there is a way to stomp all over them:

> For God did not give us a spirit of timidity or cowardice or fear, but [He has given us a spirit] of power and of love and of sound judgment and personal discipline [abilities that result in a calm, well-balanced mind and self-control]. (2 Timothy 1:7)

When I discovered that God is not the author of fear, but rather my Source of balance and self-control, my thought life and spoken life both changed. What God does provide is the Holy Spirit through whom we are conditioned with a calmness and comfort that are heaven-sent. That doesn't mean that every fear I have suddenly dissipates, but it does mean that I can make my choices based on sound judgment and not on worry or cowardice. This requires very conscious thoughts and prayers so that I can weed out any lies I might still be believing. Spending quiet time in God's presence not only brings life-joy to my soul, but it calms my anxiety so that I can think clearly. One of the most important lessons I've learned is to rehearse scripture that reminds fear Who is boss:

- ***God strengthens us:*** "Do not fear [anything], for I am with you; Do not be afraid, for I am your God. I will strengthen you, be assured I will help you; I will certainly take hold of you with My righteous right hand [a hand of justice, of power, of victory, of salvation]." (Isaiah 41:10)
- ***God is with us:*** "Have I not commanded you? Be strong and courageous! Do not be terrified or dismayed (intimidated), for the Lord your God is with you wherever you go." (Joshua 1:9)

- ***God is faithful:*** "But the Lord is faithful, and He will strengthen you [setting you on a firm foundation] and will protect and guard you from the evil one." (2 Thessalonians 3:3)
- ***God helps us:*** "So we take comfort and are encouraged and confidently say, 'The Lord is my Helper [in time of need], I will not be afraid. What will man do to me?'" (Hebrews 13:6)

Passing on fears to our children is also sadly easier than we think. They watch us so closely, listen to everything we say, emulate us, and want to be like us when they grow up. We don't have to pretend we have it all together, but we do need to model a life that does not focus on fear. To stop fear from taking control of generation after generation, God wants us to lean into His strength and victory over fear and trust Him in every situation we face. When we look to Him for reassurance of our identity, fear of rejection gets thrown out. When we allow Him to strengthen us in our weakness, He gets the glory He deserves. When we trust in His sovereign will, the fear of missing out is moot; this includes whether Alex suddenly dies or not—God is in control. When we ask the God of angel armies to protect us, we fear no more for safety. That doesn't guarantee that accidents won't happen, but it sets our minds at ease because we know God has a plan that is not limited by our sight.

As I mentioned regarding depression, sometimes medication can help with anxiety, and again, there is no shame in using it as a source of help. At the same time, the more we know the God of the Bible and His faithfulness to past generations, the more we can trust Him with ours and future generations. When our faith meets our choice to depend on God's victorious right hand, "God's wonderful peace that transcends human understanding" eliminates the fear of the unknown and teaches us to walk every day in a calm, well-balanced life (Philippians 4:7, TPT). Fear ends here.

## Choice Challenge

What are you afraid of? What lies of the enemy cause you to fear the most? Would you like God's help to wipe out your fears and anxieties? Will you let Him? Remember, your choice of faith over fear matters not just today, but for the generations that come after you. Will you choose to depend on His strength in battle so He can liberate you from your fears? Write down the three things that cause you the most fear, and then give them up to the control and protection of your Champion Jesus.

## Prayer

*Dear Father, my fears often get the better of me, but I know You are bigger than all of them. Please wash me clean of their stains and set me free from their bondage. Will You help me choose to release my anxieties and worries and trust You to fight for me in battle? I choose to believe You are my True Champion, the Author of my faith. In Jesus' name, Amen.*

# Part IV

# Choosing True Life Inspires Connection & Vision

When I was first writing this book in 2022, I was also inspired with song lyrics.

My song, entitled "Your Eyes," came not only out of my closeness with Christ, but out of the fullness and peace I felt looking into His "eyes," which allowed me to not only follow in His surrendered footsteps, but to also give all of myself to His purposes:

There is a love within Your eyes /
Utter abandon, selfless focus
A life offered in full surrender / Your greatest gift for us
Your scarred hands held open / Your smile breaks through
to my aching heart / It's all You, it's all You.

Holy, You are holy / Faithful, You are faithful
A balm to my broken / A comfort within reach
An ocean I soak in / Only safety underneath
Behind Your eyes / I could never deny
You wait for me to find / Your relentless love alive.

There is a home I've come to know /
A tranquil glass sea flowing brightly
Peace that passes all understanding /
You hold my heart so tightly
My Jesus' hands open / My Jesus' smile too
The answer I seek / It's all You, it's all You

I've been waiting, quiet, alert /
hoping for acceptance, the good, the bad, the dirt
Suddenly Your eyes pierce through /
I discover Truth, I uncover You[41]

41 Compton, Holly J. "Your Eyes," original song, 2022.

Chapter 10

# COMMUNITY

Now that the Holy Spirit is living within you, life will be a-changing! That may include your perspectives on world-implicating issues. So it's time to seek God's wisdom in His Word and perhaps new mentors or advisors for advice, especially in delicate concerns that have caused division even in the church. One of my favorite pastors, Jon Adams, used to always say, "Major in the majors, and minor in the minors."[42] In other words, we can agree that Jesus is the Son of God who lived a perfect life, died to pay the penalty for our sins, and was resurrected for us so we could forever know God. However, we should not harp on the less urgent aspects of Christianity, like whether you now should be baptized as an adult and/or by full immersion rather than being sprinkled as a baby. Stick to the most important stuff, focusing on loving one another rather than on who is right.

All that to say, before you make any major, life-altering choices, seek out God's wisdom and advice from fellow Christians, remembering to guard your heart in

42 Jon Adams, pastoral teaching at The Vine Community Church, Cumming, GA, personal communication.

relationships with nonbelievers who might try to sway your happily open mind.

You know, we were never meant to be alone. We were created for companionship. It should not be our objective to rely only on ourselves. Our lives were meant to be shared and woven together with those around us like an intricate tapestry. Sweet friends are such a treasure, as long as we are careful to choose the right ones. We are also commanded by God to carry one another's burdens. So choosing to walk the *water*-to-*wine* road includes joining the body of Christ in a local church.

And finally, believe it or not, being a Christian isn't about what you can get out of God or other people. Love is a two-way street. But do not fear, my friend. You don't have to be an evangelist unless that's the gift you believe God gave you. God wants us to be motivated by compassion to use our gifts and abilities to love others the way He loves them: by caring for their needs.

## Choice #26 – Alone or Along?

In 2012, I led a seven-person team on a mission trip to Haiti. On the last day of our trip, our team hopped on the back of a flatbed truck surrounded by a steel cage and headed up to the top of a nearby mountain to host a worship service for a small community. Now the truck was two hours late to pick us up, so we were two hours late to start the service, and two hours late to finish it. When midnight hit, we hopped into our steel "pumpkin" and began the hour-long ride back to campus. However, only five minutes in, the truck blew a tire. So in the dark of night, we climbed out of our cage and hung out on the side of the road for two more hours while the men and driver attempted to fix it.

Meanwhile, I'm standing there with our team members, tarantulas (yikes!), and several Haitian friends and children who were along for the ride. I have all our passports and the remainder of the money we brought with us. My mind was freaking out a little bit because we had very little protection should someone come along and want to rob us. I had pulled everything out of the campus safe earlier that day because we were leaving early the next morning. We all just prayed for God's angel armies to protect us until the truck was ready.

A more ominous threat, however, was inching its way closer and closer during those frightening few hours. From the top of the mountain, we watched a tropical storm roll over the mountain peaks, poised to hit us at any moment, just as the men finished changing the tire. We piled back into our steel cage during the calm before the storm. Terrified, we sat on metal bleachers on the flatbed and took off down the mountain. Within minutes, we began getting pelted with surprisingly icy cold rain. Most of us had not brought jackets, umbrellas, or any covering at all. I just sat there with my arms wrapped around myself, head down, bent over, drowning, freezing. My body just didn't know what to do with that. My mind, either! I was in such a state of shock that all I could do was cry. A deep, almost wailing cry came over me; I truly felt like I could die, if not from being struck by lightning, then by hypothermia.

That's when my dear friend Libby came over to me and wrapped her arms around my frigid body. She is the only one who did have a poncho; we called her the "MacGyver" of mission trips—she was always prepared! She offered her body to warm mine for the first few minutes, then her husband Devin joined us, sandwiching me between them. They held me tightly until my core finally thawed. By the time we got back to campus about 3:00 a.m., we were laughing and enjoying ourselves as the rain continued to fall. Thankfully, the storm dissipated as it passed overnight with minimal damage. Libby and Devin had saved my life, and I will be forever grateful.

During that experience, I realized more than ever that God did not create Adam and stop there. He created Eve, too. We were never created to be alone. We were created to live in community with one another. Writing to the Corinthians, Paul said, "For just as the body is one and yet has many parts, and all the parts, though many, form [only] one body, so it is with Christ" (1 Corinthians 12:12). As the "body" of Christ, together we make up the many parts of a body, and each part is as necessary as another. God created us to need each other in this way, just as I needed Libby and Devin in Haiti. What a grand experience I would have missed out on if I hadn't taken the lead for that team! That was my part. Devin and Libby had theirs, too; without them, we'd either still be stranded on that mountaintop or possibly dead!

When Paul wrote to the Ephesians regarding community, he urged them to choose life in their behavior towards one another through loving actions, peaceful self-control, and gratitude, thus allowing the Holy Spirit to unify them as one body:

> So I, the prisoner for the Lord, appeal to you to live a life worthy of the calling to which you have been called [that is, to live a life that exhibits godly character, moral courage, personal integrity, and mature behavior—a life that expresses gratitude to God for your salvation], with all humility [forsaking self-righteousness], and gentleness [maintaining self-control], with patience, **bearing with one another in [unselfish] love**. Make every effort to keep the **oneness of the Spirit in the bond of peace [each individual working together to make the whole successful**]. There is **one body [of believers]** and **one Spirit**—just as you were called to one hope when called [to salvation]—one Lord, one faith, one baptism, one God and Father of us all who is [sovereign] over all and [working] through all and [living] in all. Yet **grace [God's undeserved favor] was given to each one of us** [not indiscriminately, but in different ways] in proportion to the measure of Christ's [rich and abundant] gift. (Ephesians 4:1-7, emphasis added)

He called on every individual person to combine their efforts to make the one body function appropriately. He emphasized that this is done by the grace of God, allowing for each body part to be different and yet perform seamlessly as a whole. God said it was not good for Adam to be alone, so He made Eve to complement him. So it is still with believers today—separate, but of one mind, with unselfish love, gracefully working together and blessing one another. This calls for an intentional choice of humility with understanding that we are in this life together and should treat each other with focused mercy, just as Jesus does for us:

> Do nothing from selfishness or empty conceit [through factional motives, or strife], but with [an attitude of] humility [being neither arrogant nor self-righteous], regard others as more important than yourselves. Do not merely look out for your own personal interests, but also for the interests of others. (Philippians 2:3-4)

We are not born into such attitudes toward other people. We'd prefer to compete for number one, having our interests addressed first, our motives not questioned, and our singular paths unaltered by others. The *water-into-wine* path is not a path for one person alone; it starts that way, but when we arrive at our heavenly destination, our celebratory life will be caught up with the multitudes who have gone before us. So here and now on earth, we are meant to serve one another, to need one another along this journey. Proverbs 27:17 (TPT) says, "It takes a grinding wheel to sharpen a blade, and so one person sharpens the character of another." How can a blade be sharpened without a grinding wheel? And how can we survive this life overburdened by the baggage we carry, should we be alone?

Paul admonishes us again: "Carry one another's burdens and in this way you will fulfill the requirements of the law of Christ [that is, the law of Christian love]" (Galatians

6:2). When one part of the body suffers with sorrow, the whole body mourns together. When one part of the body is honored, the whole body rejoices together. In this way, we "do life" together, not a single part more valuable than another, not a single part unnecessary or unwanted. We do not have to walk this life alone. This is how we choose life in community.

## Choice Challenge

Are you a part of a body of believers in Jesus? Why, or why not? You are an essential part of the body of Christ, whether you have discovered what part you play yet or not. Will you choose to join a body, to walk the *water*-into-*wine* path in a community of faith? And will you look to the interest of others, in humility, by the power of God's grace at work within you? Write about some ways you can reach out to care for the needs of others in your life. (Ideas could include bringing another family a hot meal during trials, helping someone move, or just offering a well-timed, listening ear.)

## Prayer

*Dear Father, sometimes it's just easier to focus on myself or my family and our needs. Please forgive me for my selfishness, and please set me free to enjoy life in a community of believers. I lay my life at Your feet, Lord. Show me the true-life path, walking hand-in-hand with all the other parts of Your body. Sustain me so I can help carry someone else's burdens by Your grace. In Jesus' name, Amen.*

## Choice #27 – Foe or Friend?

Tony S. and I met in my very first creative writing class in high school. We became fast friends without realizing right away that he was already a friend of my brother Tony W., which wasn't really a surprise. (Although a year ahead of me in school, my brother and I ran in similar crowds.) But my friendship with Tony S. grew into much more by the end of high school, so we dated off and on during my early years of college, right about the time when my faith was just waking up. However, as my calling into ministry became clearer, I knew a certain conversation would not be far behind us.

"Jesus is my Lord and Savior, but my faith will never be more than that," Tony S. said, as I felt cracks enter my heart like splinters.

"You never see yourself attending church or in ministry of any kind?" I asked him, already knowing the answer. We had had long email exchanges about God and issues of faith, but my heart begged for a different answer anyway. Even a "someday" would have sufficed.

"No, Holly." The words echoed in my silent bedroom, as my wounded reality welled up my tears. I just couldn't understand why God would put him in my life and bring us together if we weren't meant to be.

"I just see myself being in ministry with my husband," I told him.

We sat motionless, the disappointment suffocating.

"We both believe in Jesus, Holly. Isn't that enough?"

"It's not, Tony." I couldn't say any more. I didn't want to throw Bible verses in his face, and I didn't have to. He knew me well enough to know I was serious about my direction in life. And just like that, I lost one of my best friends, because I knew. I knew what I was called to do. And I needed a like-spirited, soul-tending partner. And Tony S. wasn't him.

At some point as a young Christian, I became familiar with the phrase "unequally bound" from 2 Corinthians 6:14 in reference to believers being in partnership with nonbelievers:

> Do not be unequally bound together with unbelievers [do not make mismatched alliances with them, inconsistent with your faith]. For what partnership can righteousness have with lawlessness? Or what fellowship can light have with darkness?

While this verse was originally speaking about business relationships, the root of the truth applies to marriage, too. This was a tough truth to face in several relationships when it became clear that the person I was dating was a Christian in words only. Although they were "believers" according to *their* standards, a partnership with them would be painfully challenging. I didn't want to be a nag-and-drag wife, the one insisting our family attend church or read the Bible together and pray. Ultimately, conflicting worldviews would affect our abilities to raise our children in agreement or make any important decision through mutual surrender to the Lord's will. We would face an ongoing battle over how we spent our time, how we spent our money, what kind of friends to keep, and so much more that I couldn't even foresee at the time. One of us would have to lose in every fight, and that's no way to fuel a healthy marriage.

On the other hand, my husband Alex and I have the same calling and depth of faith. This was obvious to me from the moment we met. Because both of us had submitted our lives to Jesus, we already knew that our worldviews aligned, our standards the same, so our spirits were free to connect on the deepest level. Choosing a partner with not just the same faith but the same life purpose sets us up for the *wine* life in marriage, making it possible to enjoy the adventurous journey and grow together in the pursuit of transformation. Together we could leave behind the nag-and-drag *water* life because we know there is a better way.

What a blessing to know that God guides our choices in this area so that He can provide the right "match." Seeing outside of time, He views our entire lifetime of mutual surrender to, worship of, and obedience to Him, which allows His blessings to flow freely over such couples. Proverbs 18:22 (TPT) says, "When a man finds a wife, he has found a treasure! For she is the gift of God to bring him joy and pleasure." Praise the Lord for such a wonderful, sovereign God whom we can trust in this area of our lives!

Now, in regard to the wording of 2 Corinthians 6:14, I believe the same standard can be applied to all relationships in our lives—general friendships, mentoring relationships, and even business partnerships, as I mentioned. We are warned against mismatched "alliances" of any kind:

> Don't become partners with those who reject God. How can you make a partnership out of right and wrong? That's not partnership;

> that's war. Is light best friends with dark? Does Christ go strolling with the Devil? Do trust and mistrust hold hands? Who would think of setting up pagan idols in God's holy Temple? But that is exactly what we are, each of us a temple in whom God lives. God himself put it this way: "I'll live in them, move into them; I'll be their God and they'll be my people. So leave the corruption and compromise; leave it for good," says God. "Don't *link up* with those who will *pollute* you. I want you all for myself. I'll be a Father to you; you'll be sons and daughters to me." (2 Corinthians 6:14-18, MSG, emphasis added)

Sometimes we are not aware of the "partnerships" that we have in our lives, and so we unwittingly become influenced by others' worldviews, mindsets, and goals in ways we don't anticipate or fight against. God calls us to a higher standard regarding the friends we keep and the people we work with, whether it be in a workplace, in ministry, and even at home. If there are negative influences in our lives—meaning any significant relationship where there is not mutual surrender to the Lord and His purposes—we may not realize our standards and convictions can be easily manipulated.

This is why we shouldn't "link up" with those who could "pollute" us by our own accidental consent. In most relationships, we are either being influenced by the other, or we are doing the influencing. It's essential to be aware of our position in every relationship using the wisdom of

God. Then we are able to discern and choose our position on purpose. We can choose to be influenced by a mentor, choose to influence another as a mentor ourselves, or simply find friends who are also committed to Jesus. In the latter case, you have found a true blessing: "As iron sharpens iron, so one man sharpens [and influences] another [through discussion]" (Proverbs 27:17).

This principle is true at every age and stage of life. If a relationship is characterized by chaos, this should serve as a red flag. I see this playing out in my teenage daughter's life as she deals with girls who are friends one day and ghosting enemies the next. At the same time, she has one friend she has known since first grade who has remained a constant support and source of comfort for her, although we moved during their sixth-grade year. And yes, that friend is a Christian who was recently baptized as a teenager.

In the case of business partnerships, why would you enter into a legal relationship unless you are sure of the integrity of both parties to ethically follow through on agreed terms? "Right or wrong," "trust and mistrust"—these pairings bring forth chaos and maybe even war. Just because an investment seems promising, no big decisions should be made without input from the Lord; no matter how much we surrender to the Lord, it is still easy to be swayed by worldly values.

Seeking the Lord for discernment should be an essential part of beginning a new friendship or partnership. I am blessed that Alex has that spiritual gift and can know immediately upon meeting someone if he or she is someone we can trust or not. If you do not have this gift or cannot sense it yourself, seek the advice of someone you do trust, another "iron," or a mentor who can lead you with godly wisdom.

If you happen to be in a group of non-Christian friends, please know I'm not suggesting you leave the group or end those friendships. The beautiful truth is that you now have a light inside you that they may have never seen before. Jesus said,

> You are the light of [Christ to] the world. A city set on a hill cannot be hidden; nor does anyone light a lamp and put it under a basket, but on a lampstand, and it gives light to all who are in the house. Let your light shine before men in such a way that they may see your good deeds and moral excellence, and [recognize and honor and] glorify your Father who is in heaven. (Matthew 5:14-16)

Just as someone may have been a light in your life, you now have the opportunity to do so for others. God has placed certain people in your life at this current stage for a reason, and extending His love and grace to those people is now part of who you are becoming.

Sometimes we may go from one season to the next without realizing what kind of influence we have on people. Tony S. eventually began living a true life of faith with his wife, Lisa. He died of cancer in 2019 and is now in the arms of His one Lord and Savior, Jesus Christ. Lisa told me that Tony S. attributed his saving faith to his relationship with me.

## Choice Challenge

Are there unequal relationships in your life that are not submitted to the authority of Christ? Do you need to step away from a relationship to avoid negative influences? Will you seek God's wisdom to know what to do in those circumstances? Journal your choice. Then come back to that journal entry after you have followed through on your choice, and write about your experience.

## Prayer

*Dear Father, I want to honor You in every relationship I have in my life. Please give me discernment to know if any relationships are unhealthy or negatively influencing my life or faith. Give me eyes to see people how You see them. Give me Your wisdom so that I might be "iron" and "light" for someone else. Thank You, Lord, for Your hand and leading in this area. In Jesus' name, Amen.*

## Choice #28 – Quiet or Quickened?

Earlier, I shared how I met Pat Wautlet in June 2004 as Alex and I went on our first ever mission trip together. As a newly engaged couple, we were excited to work as a team in this way. And we were both in awe of our team leader, Pat, whose passion for the women of Peru was obvious in every word and action. As I observed her ministry to them, her compassion pouring out on them like a warm, radiant cloud of light, I realized how disengaged my own emotions were from my mind. I had come to Peru out of a deep love for God, but somehow that love did not translate into abundant compassion for His Peruvian people.

What I knew in my mind was that Alex and I were doing what we were meant to do, whether my heart could feel it or not. But I wanted so much to feel it in my soul, too. I started asking the Lord to fill me with His compassion for these women, to connect me to and motivate me by the heart of God for His children, just like Pat. I didn't want to simply operate out of duty. I prayed that His love for them would grip me so powerfully that I would choose to serve them out of merciful compassion rather than just knowing it was the right thing to do. It was a prayer I'd end up praying for nearly 15 years.

In March 2019, I had the amazing opportunity to lead a team of ballerinas from Birmingham, Alabama, on a mission trip to Peru. My favorite part of the trip was watching the ballerinas perform; what heavenly beauty I witnessed in every one of their synchronized movements through which they communicated the love and glory of God without words. These were not your casual dancers, mind you.

While still only high schoolers, they were as professionally trained as I could imagine—solidly disciplined, fantastically observant of their teacher, incredibly gifted for such glorious movements that clearly exemplified the grace of God more beautifully than words could contain. As if that wasn't enough, they loved one another with more devotion than real sisters possibly could. Their collective faith inspired me so thoroughly that my heart overflowed with awe and gratitude that God would bless Peru with the ministry of these remarkable young ladies. Their extraordinary, cohesive bond with one another, with the Father, and with the Father's heart, reminded me of the cloud of light surrounding my sweet friend Pat, only this time, it was unmistakably contagious.

Looking back, I couldn't put my finger on it, but sometime during that week, the Lord answered my 15-year-long prayer to be filled with tender compassion that I would be irrevocably compelled to share it with others—anyone, anytime, anywhere, as I am led by the Holy Spirit. Whether I tell someone my story about how Jesus changed my life or not, my actions speak louder than words ever could. How does God love His children? By knowing them and caring for their needs. That became my new definition of "missions."

The term *evangelism* seems to have a negative taste to it in our day and age. Yes, it is a calling on every Christian's life to some degree, but most people would prefer it not apply to them. I get it. But I think it's because we don't understand what evangelism really is. Theologically, one way to think of it is this:

> The essence of evangelism is the message that Jesus Christ is Lord. Evangelism is our human effort of proclaiming this message—which necessarily involves using our human communication, language, idioms, metaphors, stories, experiences, personality, emotions, context, culture, locatedness—and trusting and praying that God, in his sovereign will, will supernaturally use our human and natural means to effect his divine purposes.[43]

To put it plainly, we allow God permission to use who we are to communicate that Jesus is Lord in word and in action. That still sounds a bit scary, doesn't it? I guess it depends on how many stories you have heard of missionaries being killed for sharing the message of Christ or fantastical Billy Graham crusades around the world. For the most part, God is not necessarily calling all people to speak from a stage or to travel to a foreign land to share (and some, to die for) the gospel. So fear not.

Jesus does tell us that we are to love our neighbors as ourselves:

> [Jesus asked,] "Which of these three do you think proved himself a neighbor to the man who encountered the robbers?" He answered, "The one who showed compassion and mercy to him." Then Jesus said to him, "Go and constantly do the same." (Luke 10:36-37)

43 Chan, Sam. *Evangelism in a Skeptical World: How to Make the Unbelievable News about Jesus More Believable*. Zondervan, 2018.

When Jesus told the story of the Good Samaritan, He emphasized the importance of showing compassion and mercy to our neighbors. Emotions affect little unless they serve as motivation for pouring out love on others in tangible ways. Compassion in action is the same kind of evangelism that Jesus Himself did while on earth:

- ***Compassion for the sick:*** "When He went ashore, He saw a large crowd, and felt [profound] compassion for them and healed their sick." (Matthew 14:14)
- ***Compassion for the disabled:*** "Moved with compassion, Jesus touched their eyes; and immediately they regained their sight and followed Him [as His disciples]." (Matthew 20:34)
- ***Compassion for the lost:*** "When He saw the crowds, He was moved with compassion and pity for them, because they were dispirited and distressed, like sheep without a shepherd. Then He said to His disciples, 'The harvest is [indeed] plentiful, but the workers are few. So pray to the Lord of the harvest to send out workers into His harvest.'" (Matthew 9:36-38)

Jesus' plan from the beginning was to send His "workers" into the world to harvest all the seeds that were ever sown in people's lives through compassion and mercy. He modeled the way for us to do it by caring for the physical and spiritual needs of those whom He loved. Very real, tangible needs are much easier to see than the needs of the heart, but that is how Jesus would *begin* to connect with people—the point of their physical need, whether that be healing the sick, feeding the poor, or clothing a neighbor.

Then He would welcome them into His fold, to be the Shepherd of their hearts, too:

- ***With Truth and sincerity***: "Little children (believers, dear ones), let us not love [merely in theory] with word or with tongue [giving lip service to compassion], but in action and in truth [in practice and in sincerity, because practical acts of love are more than words]." (1 John 3:18)
- ***With mercy and humility:*** "You are always and dearly loved by God! So robe yourself with virtues of God, since you have been divinely chosen to be holy. Be merciful as you endeavor to understand others, and be compassionate, showing kindness toward all. Be gentle and humble, unoffendable in your patience with others." (Colossians 3:12, TPT)

In this way, we can choose to model the example of Christ, clothed in His character—choosing to be kind at every turn, to be gentle in every interaction, to be a listening ear when needed, to be patient when tested, to be humble instead of proud. These are the ways we interact in community, whether in a church body or not; this is how we become the hands and feet of Jesus in the physical world today and use every opportunity to welcome more people into the body of Christ. These are also the choices we pass down to our children who in turn will express the message of Jesus in their own way—maybe even as ballerinas, who, just by dancing in His splendor and glory, share the truth that "The Lord is merciful and gracious, slow to anger and abounding in compassion and lovingkindness" (Psalm 103:8).

St. Francis of Assisi is commonly misattributed for the reflection on evangelism that says, "Preach the gospel at all times. Use words if necessary."[44] While the quote never appeared in St. Francis' writings, we understand its implication that our actions speak louder than words. However, 2 Timothy 4:2 tells us that it is important to know the gospel well enough to communicate it verbally should any moment require it. We share Christ's love by example, but we still know that it is impossible to share the full, consequential gospel message that transforms lives without words.

St. Francis is also often credited[45] with the following, known as the "Peace Prayer of St. Francis":[46]

> Lord, make me an instrument of your peace:
> where there is hatred, let me sow love;
> where there is injury, pardon;
> where there is doubt, faith;
> where there is despair, hope;
> where there is darkness, light;
> where there is sadness, joy.
>
> O divine Master, grant that I may not so much seek
> to be consoled as to console,

44 Galli, Mark. "Myths of St. Francis." *Christianity Today*, Aug. 2008.

45 "Peace Prayer of St. Francis," commonly misattributed; original source anonymous, first published 1912 in *La Clochette* ("The Little Bell").

46 "Peace Prayer." *Loyola Press*, www.loyolapress.com/catholic-resources/prayer/traditional-catholic-prayers/saints-prayers/peace-prayer-of-saint-francis/. Accessed 13 Nov. 2025.

to be understood as to understand,
to be loved as to love.
For it is in giving that we receive,
it is in pardoning that we are pardoned,
and it is in dying that we are born to eternal life.
Amen.

Once again, we encounter a prayer that is fully a matter of surrender and obedience, choices that are passed on to the generations. If we seek to console rather than be consoled, we are putting the needs of others before our own; that is the message of the gospel itself—that "No one has greater love [nor stronger commitment] than to lay down his own life for his friends" (John 15:13). Thus, we can only become "instrument[s] of [His] peace" when we acknowledge that His way is better than our own, that His model of compassion is poured out in the everyday occurrences that fall in the *water* category and need help making it into the *wine* category. This prayer implies that we have the eyes of Jesus so that we can see the needs placed before us and choose to meet those needs in humility.

And rest easy, my friend, if you're wondering about traveling abroad to do missions in a foreign land where you don't speak their language. Should God actually call you to the mission field, you will see how God's language of sacrificial lovingkindness is universal.

## Choice Challenge

Does the word *evangelism* scare you? Forget that word. How about *compassion*? Do you have Jesus' heart for helping others at the point of their need? That's all you need. If not, will you ask Him for His heart? When He answers, will you choose to walk it out and model that compassion for others? Write down some ways you can show Christ's mercy to those outside your inner circle of family/friends. (Perhaps get to know your neighbors and identify their needs, or strike up a caring conversation with the person sitting next to you on an airplane.)

## Prayer

*Dear Father, I want to have Your heart for all those who are in need. Will You please fill me with Your compassion and help me live Your model of lovingkindness and mercy? Please help me choose to faithfully share Your message with those whom You bring into my life. And if necessary, give me the words to tell them Who You are. In Jesus' name, Amen.*

Chapter 11

# TRUST

I love that God is into details. I don't know if He chose that singular fly to buzz around my head while I'm writing, but I do know He's the God that set the stars in the sky and the planets in their courses and the atmosphere just so, and He planted the trees and plants in the ground for us to breathe in their oxygen so they could breathe in our carbon dioxide. And this Creator of the universe loves ME and wants to know ME personally. What?! I love that He likes to show off His creativity through all the different, 100% unique people in this crazy world, not to mention the countless examples of beauty and grandeur that surround us in the great outdoors! He does *not* disappoint!

God also sees the Big Picture, and the great part is, He sees all, knows all, and is everywhere all at once. Nothing gets past Him. There are no secrets. Having created all things, He maintains control so that we don't have to. That spells freedom, for me at least! So when it comes to you and me, He has plans for us that might just blow our minds if we knew it all. The best part is that we can fully entrust our plans and dreams to His capable hands.

While the popular belief that the Bible says "Do not fear" 365 times (one for every day of the year) is not entirely accurate, the Scriptures do tell us not to be afraid in hundreds of varying ways, emphasizing the fact that fear should not keep us from living life but should cause us to look to God with trust instead. I think it's exciting to read many of those instructions to not fear as they usually precede God showing up, taking the reins, and bringing the victory! So we have this choice to either let fear keep us from taking risks or dreaming big, or we can choose faith in a perfect, in-control (sovereign), 100%-loving Father to take care of it all.

## Choice #29 – Trying or Trusting?

I have a plaque on the wall in my office that reminds me that I'm being watched at all times—not in a stalker way, but in God's way of empathetic kindness—which says: "Then she called the name of the LORD who spoke to her, 'You are God Who Sees'; for she said, 'Have I not even here [in the wilderness] remained alive after seeing Him [who sees me with understanding and compassion]?'" (Genesis 16:13). This kind of compassion is God's motivation for walking with us all the days of our lives. His great love, offered freely, without obligation, is thus *our* motivation for trusting Him to do what His Word says He will do. As we know Him more and more, our trust grows exponentially. We simply have to let Him in. In Ann Voskamp's book *Waymaker*, she says:

> When God knocks and moves right in, dwells within, abides within, takes up residence and makes His home within, takes off His shoes, lights a candle, leans over and slips His arm around you, the Way has already found you,

> and you are home where you're emotionally known and forever soul-safe. Why need a way to somewhere else when your interior world with the WayMaker is so lovely, so enfolded in a love where ***you are fully seen*** and ***deeply known*** and ***wholly safe***, a world you can turn and return to, when there is nowhere else you want to be?[47]

This is what I see in Jesus' eyes, a knowing that is so complete where there is only safety, total acceptance, and full love. Why would we not trust a love like that?

While my dad was alive, I didn't know that kind of love from him. We had a difficult relationship well into adulthood. By the time he passed away, we had found mutual reconciliation but not the closeness I had always hoped for. Then, on the five-year anniversary of his death, I had a dream about him unlike any I'd had before. We were in my favorite clothing store, and I asked him why he was there. "So I can watch over you," is all he said. But as I looked into his ***eyes***, I heard so much more. In that moment, I saw ***Jesus' eyes*** looking back at me. *That* look, that look of *unconditional* love—an all-knowing, all-accepting, all-open, all-desiring, all-encompassing look that says, "I love you more than you could ever know"—without any thought of judgment or self-interest. Jesus was welcoming me into a relationship with God's very heart through the eyes of my earthly father.

47 Voskamp, Ann. *Waymaker: Finding the Way to the Life You've Always Dreamed Of.* W Publishing Group, 2022, emphasis added.

This was also a father-daughter moment of restoration with my earthly dad. In all my dreams of him before this, I'd never really looked into his eyes like that. "Looked" is not quite the right word for it; this time was like feeling his heavenly soul—whole, new, vibrant, restored, at rest. In just one glance, as if for the first time in our lives, we understood each other, and I was forever changed and have never stopped feeling genuinely close to my dad. There was healing and peace in this that redeemed some of my deepest wounds.

Jesus offers us this kind of closeness, too, one that inspires hope and a bond of trust. So if we have already invited Jesus to be our Lord and Savior, our next step is putting our trust in Him to keep His promises. The Word is very specific about how we are to trust Him with our entire being—with our hearts, with our plans, with our dreams, with our bodies, with our finances—everything is included:

- ***Submitting heart, mind, and body:*** "Trust in and rely confidently on the Lord with all your heart and do not rely on your own insight or understanding. In all your ways know and acknowledge and recognize Him, and He will make your paths straight and smooth [removing obstacles that block your way]. Do not be wise in your own eyes; fear the Lord [with reverent awe and obedience] and turn [entirely] away from evil. It will be health to your body [your marrow, your nerves, your sinews, your muscles—all your inner parts] and refreshment (physical well-being) to your bones." (Proverbs 3:5-8)

- ***Submitting plans, dreams, and finances:*** "Commit your works to the Lord [submit and trust them to Him], and your plans will succeed [if you respond to His will and guidance]." (Proverbs 16:3)

Choosing our own paths without direction from the Lord keeps us living the *water* life, but choosing to *respond to His will and guidance* results in successfully living the *wine* life. True wisdom is found in the Lord alone. Recognizing that wisdom when it comes and choosing to follow it is trusting that whatever the Lord has planned for us is better than anything we could come up with.

God is not the kind of Father who is going to drag and force us kicking and screaming down His path. He is a kind, empathetic, gentle Father who lovingly holds out His hand and says, *Trust me; I know where you need to go.* Sometimes the active choice of obedience is the open door He needs to show us the path:

> I hear the Lord saying, "I will stay close to you, instructing and guiding you along the pathway for your life. I will advise you along the way and lead you forth with ***my eyes*** as your guide. So don't make it difficult; don't be stubborn when I take you where you've not been before. Don't make me tug you and pull you along. Just come with me!" (Psalm 32:8-9, TPT, emphasis added)

Because the Father is eternal, able to see the past, present, and future all at once, and He intentionally created us with a divine purpose, we should defer to Him to make that purpose clear to us as each day of our lives unfolds. The cliche is actually true—where God guides, He also provides. He's eager to hear our prayers and requests and answer them, not as a genie in a bottle that we can command, but in ways we don't always see, but sincerely need. He is trustworthy to go before us and prepare the way.

- ***He sustains:*** "Behold, the eye of the Lord is upon those who fear Him [and worship Him with awe-inspired reverence and obedience], on those who hope [confidently] in His compassion and lovingkindness, to rescue their lives from death and keep them alive in famine." (Psalm 33:18-19)
- ***He watches:*** "God isn't blind. He who made the eye has superb vision, and he's watching all you do." (Psalm 94:9, TPT)
- ***He responds:*** "For the eyes of the Lord are [looking favorably] upon the righteous (the upright), and His ears are attentive to their prayer (eager to answer)." (1 Peter 3:12)

I have seen the eyes of Jesus in my dreams many times, even in some faces I don't necessarily recognize. But each time I *know* it is Jesus looking right at me. In each dream I am profoundly struck with this understanding that Jesus, while fully focused on me, is not concerned at all about Himself—nothing a regular human could truly say (we are all somewhat self-centered, whether we like it or not). And every time, His eyes simply say, *I'm yours; you're Mine. I see you for who you are and love you with completeness, without exception, with all that I am and all that I have to offer you. I am your safe place. I am your home.*

Allow me to summarize with this:

## Seven Reasons Why God is Trustworthy

1. **God is Always Faithful.**

   God consistently keeps His promises. The Bible is filled with examples of His faithfulness—even when people are not faithful to Him. However, He does enjoy pouring out His favor and blessing on those who are.

   - ***He is constant:*** "Therefore know [without any doubt] and understand that the Lord your God, He is God, the faithful God, who is keeping His covenant and His [steadfast] lovingkindness to a thousand generations with those who love Him and keep His commandments." (Deuteronomy 7:9)
   - ***His consistency gives us joy:*** "But I have trusted and relied on and been confident in Your lovingkindness and faithfulness; my heart shall rejoice and delight in Your salvation." (Psalm 13:5)

2. **God Always Sees What We Can't.**

   Our understanding is limited, but God sees the full picture. He knows what lies ahead and works for our ultimate good, even when things feel hard or unclear to us. Trusting in God gives us the best shot at success in our lives, especially when we are obedient to His direction and commands.

   - ***He thinks differently:*** "For my thoughts about mercy are not like your thoughts, and my ways are different from yours. As high as the heavens are above the earth, so my ways and my thoughts are higher than yours." (Isaiah 55:8-9, TPT)

- ***He has the best plan:*** "Here's what Yahweh says to you: 'I know all about the marvelous destiny I have in store for you, a future planned out in detail. My intention is not to harm you but to surround you with peace and prosperity and to give you a beautiful future, glistening with hope.'" (Jeremiah 29:11, TPT)

3. **God is Always Good.**

   God's character is pure and loving. He doesn't manipulate, deceive, or abandon. Trusting Him means leaning into a goodness that never fails.

   - ***He blesses our trust:*** "O taste and see that the Lord [our God] is good; How blessed [fortunate, prosperous, and favored by God] is the man who takes refuge in Him." (Psalm 34:8)
   - ***He is perfect:*** "If you then, evil (sinful by nature) as you are, know how to give good and advantageous gifts to your children, how much more will your Father who is in heaven [perfect as He is] give what is good and advantageous to those who keep on asking Him." (Matthew 7:11)

4. **God is in Always Control.**

   Even in chaos, God is sovereign. Trusting Him brings peace, because you're no longer carrying the pressure to control everything yourself. What a relief that we don't have to "have it all together," right? It might look like some people on the outside do have it all figured out, but truthfully, no one does. That's great news to me and my tired heart!

- ***He is capable:*** "And we know [with great confidence] that God [who is deeply concerned about us] causes all things to work together [as a plan] for good for those who love God, to those who are called according to His plan and purpose." (Romans 8:28)
- ***He knows all things:*** "For I am Wisdom, and I am shrewd and intelligent. I have at my disposal living-understanding to devise a plan for your life." (Proverbs 8:12, TPT)

5. **Jesus Proved God's Always-Love.**

The cross is the ultimate reason to trust God. He didn't stay distant from our pain—He entered into it as Jesus, who suffered and overcame it, all to bring us back to Himself. There is nothing selfish about Jesus' love for us. We can't say that about any other human who has ever walked this earth. Jesus' love does not demand anything in return. He gives without expecting it back. But He does rejoice when we return His love with trust.

- ***Jesus loves more than all:*** "No one has greater love [nor stronger commitment] than to lay down his own life for his friends." (John 15:13)
- ***God prizes us above all:*** "For God so [greatly] loved and dearly prized the world, that He [even] gave His [One and] only begotten Son, so that whoever believes and trusts in Him [as Savior] shall not perish, but have eternal life." (John 3:16)

6. **Trusting God Always Leads to Peace.**

   We can confidently expect God to come through for us because He reassures us constantly in His Word that He will do so. When we place our trust in God, we don't have to live in fear, anxiety, or despair. His presence offers us a supernatural peace.

   - ***His peace is sure:*** "You will keep in perfect and constant peace the one whose mind is steadfast [that is, committed and focused on You—in both inclination and character], because he trusts and takes refuge in You [with hope and confident expectation]." (Isaiah 26:3)
   - ***His peace transcends all:*** "Do not be anxious or worried about anything, but in everything [every circumstance and situation] by prayer and petition with thanksgiving, continue to make your [specific] requests known to God. And the peace of God [that peace which reassures the heart, that peace] which transcends all understanding, [that peace which] stands guard over your hearts and your minds in Christ Jesus [is yours]." (Philippians 4:6-7)

7. **God Never Changes.**

   Unlike people, circumstances, or emotions, God is unchanging. His character, His promises, and His love remain steady no matter what happens in the world or in our lives. That kind of stability is rare—and it's exactly why He's worthy of our trust. When everything else feels uncertain, we can anchor our hearts in the unchanging nature of God. He won't shift with trends, moods, or mistakes. His Word, His mercy, and His presence are endlessly rock-solid.

- ***He is always:*** "Jesus Christ is the same yesterday and today and forever." (Hebrews 13:8, CSB)
- ***He is finitely infinite:*** "I the Lord do not change." (Malachi 3:6, NIV)

If you're struggling to trust God right now, it's okay to start with small steps. He welcomes honesty, even in doubt. He's not asking for blind faith—He invites us into a relationship where trust grows through experience, presence, and grace. We can know that God doesn't take us to the edge of the ocean and beckon us to jump in to watch us drown; like He did for Moses and the Israelites, He brings us to that very same spot so we can watch Him part the same waters which allow us to cross safely on solid ground (read Exodus 14:21-22).

## Choice Challenge

Trusting God with your entire life is a big step of faith. Are you ready to release control to your Creator who loves you unceasingly? Can you see the unconditional acceptance in His eyes that hopes you'll take Him up on His offer? Will you trust that His plan is far better than you could ever hope or imagine? Close your eyes and envision the face of Jesus with His eyes focused on you; write down how His glance makes you feel as you bathe in His utter love and acceptance. Let that glance heal your tired soul as you release control and trust Him to hold you firmly in His grasp.

## Prayer

*Dear Father, when I close my eyes, will You give me a vision of Your all-knowing, all-loving eyes so I can trust You with my whole being? I will take Your hand and walk with You from the* water *life into the* wine *life; please help me not to drag my feet. Please speak to my heart and show me what You made me for. I am Yours, Jesus, and You are mine. I choose You, Lord. In Jesus' name, Amen.*

## Choice #30 – Big or Bigger?

When it comes to people's names, I fully believe that God is in the details. If He carves our names on the palms of His hands, then surely our names are specific, personal, and have intended meaning, just as God's name does:

> God said to Moses, "I Am Who I Am"; and He said, "You shall say this to the Israelites, 'I Am has sent me to you.'" Then God also said to Moses, "This is what you shall say to the Israelites, 'The Lord, the God of your fathers, the God of Abraham, the God of Isaac, and the God of Jacob (Israel), has sent me to you.' This is My Name forever, and this is My memorial [name] to all generations. (Exodus 3:14-15)

To me, "I Am" means, "I Am the Lord of your heart. I Am the all-knowing, all-powerful, all-present, all-pursuing God. I Am the God of your past, your present, your future. I Am the God of your parents and their parents and the God of your children and their children. I Am the sovereign God who calls you by name. I Am forever."

I am a very detail-oriented person and often tempted to take details into my own hands to manipulate them according to my liking. I like to be in control—of myself, of my surroundings, and sometimes of others. I realize that this is not God's plan. "I Am" is the God of the details. And it's His job to attend to them. Not mine.

God shows me daily that this is the case. One way He does this is through the numbers "9" and "27," which is my birthday (September 27th). Every day one way or another, that combination of numbers shows up, whether I happen to look up at the clock at exactly 9:27 or see it in a sign or a phone number, etc. Every day. It's how I know God, my God, cares about the details in my life. He calls me by name (and knows what day I was born!). I must conclude, if I can trust God with the little details, then I can trust Him with the big ones, too. In fact, I can trust "I Am" with it all.

When we get stuck in the nitty-gritty details of our lives, it becomes more difficult to see the big picture. Many times, we are stuck in the details because we like to be in control. Control is one of the three most common idols in our lives, along with security/comfort and approval. If we aren't careful, we can fall into the trap of making choices based on how much control we have over a situation rather than trusting God to attend to the details, whether big or small. The beauty of knowing the God who created the universe is the fact that we don't need to have control. We don't need to fight so hard for what we want or think we need. We don't need to hold so tightly to situations that aren't resolved so we don't lose control.

God is so much bigger than we think He is. He cannot be contained in the puny box we try to put Him in because we want things to be "just so." God wanted to tell us this, so He sent His Son to say, "I came so they can have real and eternal life, more and better life than they ever dreamed of" (John 10:10, MSG).

The Jews of Jesus' day, however, could not fathom God's eternal plan at the time. His chosen people of Israel were expecting the prophesied and long-awaited Messiah to overthrow the Roman empire that occupied their land and taxed them for Caesar. They wanted a political deliverer to reclaim David's throne, to liberate them from their Roman oppressors, and to rule over Israel once again. Jesus knew they might even try to force Him to be their king (John 6:15; Luke 24:21).

That would be considered a "puny box" for God. His plan wasn't so small that His only begotten Son would come into the physical world only to conquer Israel's current earthly enemy. Some of Jesus' disciples actually expected that, too, but the more time they spent with Jesus, the more they realized that Jesus had come to conquer their hearts, to conquer the true enemy of our souls, and to conquer death once and for all (Hebrews 2:14–15; 1 John 3:8). His followers came to understand that Christ's mission was not to restore a kingdom of this world (John 18:36) but to reign in the hearts of people everywhere for all time.

God's design for Jesus was to pay the price for the sin of every person who had ever lived and would ever live, so that all who believe in Him could return to God for a beautiful eternity. Just like us, the disciples had to release their "dream" version of the salvation they expected in order to receive the **bigger dream** of all that God intended through the Person who did, in fact, save them. After the resurrection of Jesus, the Holy Spirit helped open their eyes and hearts to what He had accomplished at the cross. Jesus was and is God's way of saying, "See, I can do so much more than you think! I hold the universe in My hands, and because I love you so much, I can give you all of it!"

- ***He knows us personally:*** "The LORD said to Moses, 'I will also do this thing that you have asked; for you have found favor (lovingkindness, mercy) in My sight and I have known you [personally] by name.'" (Exodus 33:17)

- ***He exceeds our expectations:*** "Now to Him who is able to [carry out His purpose and] do superabundantly more than all that we dare ask or think [infinitely beyond our greatest prayers, hopes, or dreams], according to His power that is at work within us..." (Ephesians 3:20)
- ***He is generous and all-knowing:*** "Every godly one receives even more than what they ask for. For you hear what their hearts really long for, and you bring them your saving strength." (Psalm 145:19, TPT)
- ***He satisfies every need:*** "I am convinced that my God will fully satisfy every need you have, for I have seen the abundant riches of glory revealed to me through Jesus Christ!" (Philippians 4:19, TPT)

For us to receive what we ask of the Lord, He simply asks for a heart that trusts Him to provide it. This liberates us, not only to ask for our smallest needs, but to ask for the ***big*** ones, too. We can release control to Him, worship Him for the supreme God He is, and trust that He is able to do so much more than all of our prayers, hopes, and dreams combined.

- ***We need Him***: "God knows what we need and can always be trusted to provide it. And by giving us our daily bread, God is teaching us a deeper lesson. He wants us to learn that what we really need is himself."[48]

---

48 Philip Graham Ryken qtd. in David Jeremiah, "What Are We Waiting For?" *Turning Points Magazine & Devotional*, Vol. 24, no. 3, March 2022, 40.

- ***We trust Him***: "The Lord knows how to satisfy our hearts while meeting all our needs. It's not just our material needs He supplies. He takes care of us emotionally, spiritually, relationally, mentally, and eternally. One trillion dollars is nothing compared to a heart trusting God."[49]

God knows the difference between our wants and our needs. God also knows something we don't—He knows the ***BIG*** plans that He has in store for *us*. It's a good thing we *don't*, honestly. We wouldn't be able to handle it all right now. His thinking and His ways are infinitely beyond our own, and He can see the end from the beginning, right? So why wouldn't we trust a God to fulfill our greatest dreams? Why stop at dreaming big? Why not ***dream bigger***?

- ***Trust Him:*** "Blessed [fortunate, prosperous, and favored by God] is the man who makes the Lord his trust." (Psalm 40:4a)
- ***Submit to Him:*** "Commit your works to the Lord [submit and trust them to Him], And your plans will succeed [if you respond to His will and guidance]." (Proverbs 16:3)
- ***Obey Him:*** "The irony of obedience is like a delicate dance of trust. It may require real sacrifice from us, while somehow leading to blessing and incomparable abundance."[50]

The greatest peace we can find, the life-joy we seek, comes when we dream bigger than we ever thought but

49 David Jeremiah, "What Are We Waiting For?" *Turning Points Magazine & Devotional*, Vol. 24, no. 3, March 2022, 40.

50 Shirer, *Discerning the Voice of God.*

do not feel compelled to make those dreams come to pass. There's a peace in not striving, a supernatural peace in the believing that God does have our best interest at heart. Remember Psalm 37:4? When it says "Delight yourself in the Lord, and He will give you the desires and petitions of your heart," it means that we choose to allow the Lord to adjust our hearts so His delights become our delights, too. That means we also choose to trust that if our dreams are God's dreams for us too, they will come to pass.

Let's be real one last time. When I was growing up and going through college, I wanted so desperately to be a musician. I had learned to play four different instruments. I loved to sing and write song lyrics; I even led worship a little and recorded songs with other singers. I enjoyed promoting concerts in Massachusetts, where I was raised, and I even considered moving to Nashville to get in on the Christian music scene. It's not that I didn't want it *enough*, didn't work hard *enough* to make it happen, or didn't dream *big* enough. It's that God had other plans for me.

As I delighted in the Lord, my desires started to change over time. God led me to Georgia where I met my husband on the day I arrived. I moved there to attend a discipleship school where one of the teachers invited me to join her on a Peru mission trip, and Alex came with me. We have three amazing kids, two of whom are already writers and very creative like me. As a family, we've spent many years ministering to the Peruvian people so that God could change lives there, and we've branched out to other countries that also need a touch of our Master's hand. Through my writing and my daughters' writing, He will reach more and more hearts so they find that beautiful eternity, too.

God had other amazing plans for me, for us...so far... But! Who's to say that I couldn't write a song or sing on a worship team or promote concerts again in the future? The Lord does like to bring things full circle. And I have it on strict authority that there will be lots of singing in heaven (check out the book of Revelation!). This former "dream" of mine, while it wasn't God's plan for me back then, it doesn't mean that the dream itself was wrong or sinful or innately bad by any means. It just means that it wasn't God's *best* plan for me at that time. If becoming a musician sometime in my future is truly going to glorify God, that's His prerogative, His choice, His plan to make.

If you have a big dream right now, I'm not telling you to give up on it. Sometimes our dreams are set on earthly desires, while His have eternity in mind. Simply delight yourself in the Lord, and allow Him to show you *His* dream.

## Choice Challenge

Do you have a big dream for your life? Something that you didn't really think was possible? Unpack that dream and give it over to the Lord, your Creator, the Originator of dreams. Will you choose to entrust those dreams to His care? Will you release control of them and trust that He's got this? I guarantee you will not be disappointed. He knows how He made you and what you truly long for, what you truly want *and* are designed for. Write down a few ways you can dream ***bigger***. Then wait and see!

## Prayer

*Dear Father, I'm scared to give up control of the details, big and small. I'm scared to hand over control of my dreams, too. But I choose to entrust it all to You, Lord, because I know You are sovereign and a good, good Father. Please take it all out of my hands and give me strength to wait on You to fulfill my every need and everything I long for. In Jesus' name, Amen.*

# Conclusion

S***urrender. Obedience.*** I pray you have been inspired to choose these ways of life in your rejuvenated walk with God. I want to encourage you to carry on in fervor. You may need to read through this book again and again. Your adventure is only just beginning. I pray you have tasted the *wine* of True Life and thirst for more of Him. I hope you have seen your choices change your world on this journey thus far. I trust that if you have made the choices your spirit has been led to make, you have also seen the blessings begin to flow in your life. If your desires have come into alignment with His and you are now clothed in the character of Christ, then you are walking the path He has called you to, and God's favor will illuminate your way ahead.

As you go, remember, too, that you are not the only human on the planet. God made us to need each other. So before I send you off, please keep this in heart, as if the Holy Spirit Himself were saying these words to you:

> Surrender your life in loyal love in pursuit of unhindered connection....You reflect my love well when you love others well. Do not isolate yourself or shut others out for fear of rejection. I made you for communion. I created you for relationship with God and with others. So

> let my love flood your heart and lead you in compassion. Even in this, my strength will cover your weakness. I will empower you to choose to support one another as you lean on my grace. Life is richer in community.[51]

Relating to others, just as with the Lord, will require the choice of surrender so that you can offer grace (TGFT!!) to everyone you meet. When you release your will to the Lord, He'll provide you with patience to give others the space to make mistakes. This is how you allow Christ's merciful compassion to flow through you every day.

When it comes to full surrender, there is one final story I'd like to share, which I first heard on that fateful mission trip in Vancouver, a story of such trust in God that it has had an unforgettable impact on my days ever since. It's the story of William Whiting Borden, the son of a wealthy Illinois family, who developed a heart for God's people while on a world tour which was a gift for his 16th birthday. Shortly after graduating from Yale University and Princeton Theological Seminary, Borden renounced his inheritance and surrendered his life to God's service. Before reaching his hopeful mission site in China, he first went to study Islam and Arabic in Cairo. There in Egypt, at the age of 25, sadly, Borden died of cerebral meningitis. While historically unsubstantiated, it was said that he wrote in his Bible these phrases: "No Reserve" after renouncing his inheritance, "No Retreat" after his father said he'd never

51 Simmons, Brian. "September 30." *I Hear His Whisper for Women.* Broadstreet Publishing Group, 2021.

work the family business, and "No Regret" shortly before he passed away.[52]

Oh, that we could all be so blessed as to live, love, and trust God with such conviction.

Allow me now to leave you with more of "Truth's shining light" (Psalm 119:105, TPT), the Word of God, to inspire you to press on in obedience, holding the hand of our friend Jesus:

- ***Be passionate and focused:*** "I admit that I haven't yet acquired the absolute fullness that I'm pursuing, but I run with passion into his abundance so that I may reach the purpose for which Christ Jesus laid hold of me to make me his own. I don't depend on my own strength to accomplish this; however I do have one compelling focus: I forget all of the past as I fasten my heart to the future instead. I run straight for the divine invitation of reaching the heavenly goal and gaining the victory-prize through the anointing of Jesus." (Philippians 3:12-14, TPT)
- ***Be compelled by grace:*** "So we're not giving up. How could we! Even though on the outside it often looks like things are falling apart on us, on the inside, where God is making new life, not a day goes by without his unfolding grace. These hard times are small potatoes compared to the coming good times, the lavish celebration prepared for us. There's far more here than meets the eye. The things we see now are here today, gone tomorrow. But the things

52 Culbertson, Howard. "William Borden — No Reserve. No Retreat. No Regrets," *SNU Homepage*, home.snu.edu/~hculbert/regret.htm.

we can't see now will last forever." (2 Corinthians 4:16-18, MSG)

- ***Be diligent:*** "So let's not allow ourselves to get fatigued doing good. At the right time we will harvest a good crop if we don't give up, or quit. Right now, therefore, every time we get the chance, let us work for the benefit of all, starting with the people closest to us in the community of faith." (Galatians 6:9-10, MSG)
- ***Be committed:*** "Therefore, since we are surrounded by so great a cloud of witnesses [who by faith have testified to the truth of God's absolute faithfulness], stripping off every unnecessary weight and the sin which so easily and cleverly entangles us, let us run with endurance and active persistence the race that is set before us, [looking away from all that will distract us and] focusing our eyes on Jesus, who is the Author and Perfecter of faith [the first incentive for our belief and the One who brings our faith to maturity], who for the joy [of accomplishing the goal] set before Him endured the cross, disregarding the shame, and sat down at the right hand of the throne of God [revealing His deity, His authority, and the completion of His work]." (Hebrews 12:1-2)
- ***Be transformed:*** "And we all, with unveiled face, continually seeing as in a mirror the glory of the Lord, are progressively being transformed into His image from [one degree of] glory to [even more] glory, which comes from the Lord, [who is] the Spirit." (2 Corinthians 3:18)

- ***Be in the Word:*** "This Book of the Law shall not depart from your mouth, but you shall read [and meditate on] it day and night, so that you may be careful to do [everything] in accordance with all that is written in it; for then you will make your way prosperous, and then you will be successful." (Joshua 1:8)
- ***Be faithful and trustworthy:*** "His master said to him, 'Well done, good and faithful servant. You have been faithful and trustworthy over a little, I will put you in charge of many things; share in the joy of your master.'" (Matthew 25:21)
- ***Be protective of your heart:*** "So above all, guard the affections of your heart, for they affect all that you are. Pay attention to the welfare of your innermost being, for from there flows the wellspring of life. Set your gaze on the path before you. With fixed purpose, looking straight ahead, ignore life's distractions. Watch where you're going! Stick to the path of truth, and the road will be safe and smooth before you. Don't allow yourself to be sidetracked for even a moment or take the detour that leads to darkness." (Proverbs 4:23, 25-27, TPT)
- ***Be obedient:*** "My child, if you truly want a long and satisfying life, never forget the things that I've taught you. Follow closely every truth that I've given you. Then you will have a full, rewarding life. Hold on to loyal love and don't let go, and be faithful to all that you've been taught. Let your life be shaped by integrity, with truth written upon your heart. That's how you will find favor and understanding

with both God and men—you will gain the reputation of living life well." (Proverbs 3:1-4, TPT)

- ***Be courageous***: "So don't lose your bold, courageous faith, for you are destined for a great reward! You need the strength of endurance to reveal the poetry of God's will and then you receive the promise in full. But we are certainly not those who are held back by fear and perish; we are among those who have faith and experience ***true life***!" (Hebrews 10:35-36, 39, TPT, emphasis added)

You are strong in faith and fully capable of the one choice you need to make every day—to follow Jesus—and the rest will take care of itself.

# Author's Note

This is part of a very personal story of God's transformative work in my life. I have by no means "arrived" at my full transformation. Many times a day, I still hear the Holy Spirit's whisper, "Choose this day Whom you will serve" (Joshua 24:15). I am constantly having to ask myself if I have fully surrendered to God or if I keep taking my life back off the sacrificial altar so I can do as I please.

In the six weeks that this book first came to life in 2022, I also walked through Priscilla Shirer's seven-week Bible study called *Discerning the Voice of God.* During that time, I had never felt so close to His heart, so open to His voice, so available to obediently follow. God faithfully filled me up with His heart of compassion for His sons and daughters so that I would understand the importance of the choices He places before us all every day of our lives. I know that intimacy with Him is something we can all find when we choose to surrender ourselves and obey His instruction from a place of humility.

While the words of this book flowed out, I understood that they were written "for such a time as this" (Esther 4:14). Suddenly, every conversation I had with friends and family geared toward this subject matter, making me think, "This person needs to read my book!" I write that with humility, knowing that I am merely a conduit of His grace for others.

My heart is simply to share the possibilities of His grace to provide hope for my reader that there really is an "abundant Life" available to all who choose True Life—Jesus—every day. I reread it when I need to preach to myself, too, in the event that I forget.

Honestly, I have tried to write this book for more than 20 years, almost my entire married life thus far. I had to wait for God's timing so that He could speak through it to the right people at His right time. I am so grateful that God will use my experiences and my writing to draw people close to Him and transform others' lives as He has mine. Thank you for joining me on this journey. May it bless you even more than it blesses me!

I invite you to meet me at HollyCompton.com where you can find more than 10 years of blog archives and current resources. Feel free to email me anytime at holly@hollycompton.com. I would love to get to know you and hear how God has been working in your life. My missions organization is at AmorRealMinistries.com where you can read about our missions work and our home for victims of domestic violence, called Pat's Place. We would love to have you join us on the mission field someday!

Lastly, I want to encourage you to read and reread this book as often as you can. Each of these 30 choices is not a choice you make once and are done. You have to wake up every day and choose again. Put your feet on the floor and surrender to His plan. You will never regret it.

www.ingramcontent.com/pod-product-compliance
Ingram Content Group UK Ltd.
Pitfield, Milton Keynes, MK11 3LW, UK
UKHW041631190726
13854UKWH00006B/2431

9 798891 853645